PLAYSCRIPT 70

shades of heathcliff

&

death of captain doughty

john spurling

MARION BOYARS · LONDON

First published in Great Britain in 1975
by Marion Boyars Publishers Ltd.,
18 Brewer Street, London, W1R 4AS

All performing rights in these plays are strictly reserved and
applications for permission to perform should be made in
advance before rehearsals to
Patricia Macnaughton
PL Representation Ltd
33 Sloane Street London SW1

No performances of the plays may be given unless a licence has
been obtained prior to rehearsal

ISBN 0 7145 2517 0 Casebound
ISBN 0 7145 2518 9 Paperbound

A MARION BOYARS BOOK
distributed by
Calder & Boyars Ltd.,
18 Brewer Street, London W1R 4AS

Typesetting by Gilbert Composing Services, Leighton Buzzard
Printed by Whitstable Litho, Kent

CONTENTS

	Page
SHADES OF HEATHCLIFF	11
DEATH OF CAPTAIN DOUGHTY	71

'In another's wine cup I make my own complaint'

Chinese Proverb

SHADES OF HEATHCLIFF

(Reminiscences of Wuthering Heights)

SHADES OF HEATHCLIFF was first performed on 8
December 1971 at Lucky's, Sheffield, by the Crucible
Theatre Vanguard Company. The play was directed by
Ed Thomason and the cast was as follows:

PONDEN	Garry McDermott
HAWORTH	Maggie McCarthy
HEBDEN	Dicken Ashworth
KEIGHLEY	Ray Ashcroft
VOICE on the TAPE	Michael Cooke

Designed and lit by Peter Barham

PART ONE

THRUSHCROSS GRANGE

1. THE PAINTING

(At the back of the stage, a large window with curtains on either side. The curtains are drawn back to reveal a large reproduction of Branwell Bronte's painting of his sisters, with holes where the faces should be. The faces are supplied by the three actors: PONDEN's face for Charlotte's, HEBDEN's for Emily's, KEIGHLEY's for Anne's.

Centre-stage, sitting on an upright chair, back to audience, facing painting, HAWORTH, dressed more or less as a boy. On her knees a manuscript in hard covers. After a pause to establish this tableau, the sound of a powerful car accelerating, then tape plays over loudspeaker)

TAPE.   Going like a bat out of hell up the fast lane, heading north at a hundred and twenty, glimpsed them for a moment—pale faces blurred behind the glass of the Trowell self-service cafeteria—three women. Was there a fourth—a callow youth, seated somewhat back of the table, or was that a trick of the light, reflection in the glass? Hard to tell, I was wearing my shades. But does the sex matter? These four will be my characters. Method of writing this book: no sitting at a desk, no fiddle-faddle with pen or typewriter. Write as you live, piloting your great torpedo of steel, wood, leather and glass. My true existence is only at the wheel, asserting my will with nonchalant brutality and unerring skill over thousands of pounds' worth of sophisticated machinery. Beneath the instrument panel, my tape-recorder; strapped to my chest, the microphone. I shall speak my book as I go, hurtling from city to city, annihilating time and space, stamping on man's history and nature's geography the broad rubber hieroglyphs of my racing radials. . .

(Lights off painting, curtains close)

2. THE MANUSCRIPT

(HAWORTH *turns her chair round, so as to face audience. Enter* PONDEN *with two cups of tea. He gives one to* HAWORTH, *seats himself near her, stirs his own cup.* HAWORTH *drops manuscript on floor between their chairs. They sip their tea in silence)*

HAWORTH.   You don't like it, do you?

(PONDEN *takes deep breath, but doesn't speak)*

What do you think is wrong with it? I wonder if you're any judge of what's wrong with it. After all, you spend your time poring over old novels, things written long ago, established classics of the English language. What would you know about something new? You wouldn't, you'd be out of your depth. You wouldn't recognise a modern masterpiece if you saw one, because you could only judge it by the standards of the past. You're a bloody second-hand, second-class academic and I couldn't care less whether you like it or not.

PONDEN.   *(After pause)* I think it's very good. The idea is good. The idea of the man in the car and the four people behind glass.

HAWORTH.   Go on.

PONDEN.   I wonder if you couldn't. . .

HAWORTH.   Yes?

PONDEN.   If you couldn't. . .the text, I mean. . .

HAWORTH.   Rewrite the whole blasted thing?

PONDEN.   No, no. What I mean is that it's slightly. . .

HAWORTH.   Go on.

PONDEN.   I was going to say: slightly. . .overblown. *(Pause)* Doesn't it here and there verge on the vulgar?

(HAWORTH *picks up manuscript, holds it for a moment as though guessing its weight, then hurls it violently at* PONDEN. *It misses him and skids across the stage)*

HAWORTH.   I'm a bloody vulgar writer and you're a bloody second-hand, second-class academic. Why don't we just go and gas ourselves?

(PONDEN *stands up and goes to her, touches her lightly on the shoulder*)

PONDEN. I used the wrong word.

(HAWORTH *breaks away from him, goes across to manuscript*)

Let me read it again, think about it and try to give you a considered opinion. For what my opinion's worth.

HAWORTH. *(Trying unsuccessfully to tear manuscript)* Vulgar, vulgar, vulgar.

PONDEN. Don't do that. Give it to me.

HAWORTH. *(Twisting away from him and still trying to tear manuscript)* Vulgar, vulgar.

PONDEN. Don't. Please don't.

(PONDEN *gets hold of manuscript, pulls, but she holds on to it and the thing tears between them*)

HAWORTH. Overblown! Vulgar! Vulgar! Vulgar! Vulgar!

(Throwing the manuscript across the stage, she kneels down, bending her head over her knees. PONDEN also kneels and tries to force her head up to look at him. They freeze in these positions)

3. INTERIOR

(HEBDEN *and* KEIGHLEY *appear stage right. They stand, or lean on chairs, as though looking through a window into the room where* PONDEN *and* HAWORTH *are kneeling on the floor*)

HEBDEN. Fitted carpet.

KEIGHLEY. Rembrandt-red, demi-pile.

HEBDEN. Three-piece Scandinavian suite.

KEIGHLEY. Scatter cushions.

HEBDEN. Off-peak central-heating units.

KEIGHLEY. Two-bar electric fire with simulated glowing coals.

HEBDEN. Best quality brass fire-irons, never used. What would they use them for?

KEIGHLEY. Natural wood standard-lamp and Copenhagen mermaid porcelain table-lamp.

HEBDEN. Hi-fi stereo record-player and double speakers.

KEIGHLEY. Black and white 21 inch television with indoor aerial.

HEBDEN. Isn't it amazing? They're fighting over an old exercise book.

KEIGHLEY. The rain's pouring down the back of my collar and between my shoulder-blades. After that it seems to get held up by the waist-band of my underpants, so it runs round my waist several times before finally finding its way down my trouser-legs and so to the ground, which it would have got to much quicker if only it hadn't made such a thing of pouring down my collar in the first place.

(HEBDEN and KEIGHLEY stare at PONDEN and HAWORTH. Suddenly HAWORTH sees them, points. PONDEN turns to look. All four freeze in these positions, while the tape plays)

TAPE: These are my characters, to do with as I like. But what shall I do with them? Give them names and characteristics, put them through some well-hedged story, like cows down a country-lane, in at one gate and out at another? Pin down relationships and motives as if they were butterflies on a card, as if there were only one answer to every question? God no! Let's admit it, these characters are mere shades of me, they have no independent existence. I'll make them live as I live, inside my plunging projectile, braking, accelerating, skidding, cornering, changing up through the five gears and down again, their pasteboard hearts pounding, their painted blood surging according to the savage rhythms of the road. . .

4. A CUP OF HOT TEA

(PONDEN and HAWORTH sit on chairs centre, HAWORTH back and right of PONDEN. They sip tea. HEBDEN and KEIGHLEY walk across and stand near them. They also carry cups of tea)

HEBDEN. Are you going near Sheffield?

PONDEN. Why?

HEBDEN. Someone was giving us a lift, but his car's broken down.

PONDEN. You want me to give you a lift?

KEIGHLEY. That's it.

HAWORTH. Yes, we could.

PONDEN. No, I don't think so.

HAWORTH. Why not?

PONDEN. I don't like the length of their hair.

HAWORTH. That's no reason.

PONDEN. If they want people to give them free transport, they should make some effort to look presentable.

HAWORTH. Mean.

PONDEN. It's my car and I don't want a couple of wet yaks in the back seat.

(HEBDEN *throws the dregs of his cup of tea in* PONDEN's *face.* PONDEN *stands up, mopping at his face and clothes with a handkerchief*)

PONDEN. Do you think behaviour of that sort is best calculated to get you a lift?

HEBDEN. I'm sorry. I lost my temper.

KEIGHLEY. You annoyed him.

(HAWORTH *takes* PONDEN's *handkerchief and mops his face*)

HEBDEN. I apologise.

PONDEN. *(Sitting down and continuing to brush himself)* Sit down. I'll give you a lift.

HAWORTH. Why should you give a lift to a pair of thugs?

PONDEN. I dislike violence.

HAWORTH. That's no reason to give way to violence.

PONDEN. I shouldn't have provoked violence. The fault was mine.

(HEBDEN *and* KEIGHLEY *bring chairs and sit down right of* PONDEN *and* HAWORTH)

HAWORTH. *(To* PONDEN) You're trembling all over.

13

KEIGHLEY. Look at that car going up the fast lane.

(They all sit staring towards audience, their positions the same as the three sisters in the painting, with HAWORTH where the pillar comes)

HAWORTH. *(After pause)* You could have knocked him down. That's what I'd have done.

(HEBDEN *smiles at* HAWORTH)

PONDEN. *(Standing up)* Shall we get going? (*To* HEBDEN) Unless you want another cup of tea?

TAPE. The incurable mediocrity of my characters. Nothing so definite as characters, my shades. Their tawdry bourgeois souls. Tantrums in teacups. Wait till I get at them. 'Once upon a time there were four nice little bunny-rabbits. . .' said the fox.

5. TWO DREAMS ON THE MOTORWAY

(The actors place their chairs two behind two, facing the audience, then sit down as if they were in a car—
PONDEN *driving,* HAWORTH *beside him,* KEIGHLEY *behind* HAWORTH, HEBDEN *behind* PONDEN, *but leaning forward so that his face appears between* PONDEN's *and* HAWORTH's *shoulders.* PONDEN *and* HAWORTH *move their right arms in concert, like windscreen wipers)*

PONDEN. Violence is simply childishness. Only children believe they can solve things by violence and this belief survives in grown men as a childhood fantasy. It's deeply rooted in all of us, this secret admiration for violence, for its magical power to change things. Even though we know rationally that it's a false satisfaction, that violence is stupid, degrading and changes nothing.

HOWARTH. All he means is, he's afraid of violence. 'Pax', he says, 'pax. Don't hit me and I won't hit you.' But he won't hit you anyway, because he doesn't need to. He's got everything he wants already: good salary, comfortable job, nice house, high-class education, social respect. Violence is the only way of changing the power-structure, but he

doesn't want it changed, because he's where the
power is.

PONDEN. The most advanced people in history are
those who have overcome the need for violence in
themselves—Socrates, Christ, Buddha, Mahatma
Ghandi. But the heroes most people admire are the
retarded sort, the sword-waving, gun-toting babies
like Alexander the Great, Julius Caesar, and
Napoleon. Even today when everybody pretends
to condemn mass-murderers like Hitler and Stalin,
they secretly admire them. You'll say we're making
some advance when people feel ashamed of
admiring them, as they feel ashamed of secret
childish vices, but it's not enough. The need for
violence is evidently a basic flaw in the human
character. The only hope is to eradicate it
biologically, we shall have to alter human nature
by scientific means. Meanwhile. . . Has it stopped
raining?

(He and HAWORTH stop moving their arms)

No.

(They move their arms again like windscreen
wipers)

HEBDEN. Meanwhile?

PONDEN. Meanwhile we shall continue to rely on
nature's primitive antidote.

HEBDEN. What's that?

PONDEN. Fear. Fear of the consequences.

(He and HAWORTH stop moving their arms)

HAWORTH.   Listen to the Anglo-Saxon white
Protestant liberal.

HEBDEN. You two are always fighting.

PONDEN. I don't fight her.

HAWORTH.   See what I mean (Looking round at
KEIGHLEY) Your friend's fallen asleep.

(Leaving KEIGHLEY leaning sideways in his chair,
the others take their chairs to opposite sides of the
stage, PONDEN to right, HAWORTH and
HEBDEN to left. HAWORTH and HEBDEN sit on

15

their chairs, PONDEN *stands on his)*

PONDEN. *(Gesticulating histrionically as though in a pulpit)* Violence is the curse of mankind. I say unto you, find a cure. The flames of European violence have already consumed two generations. Now we see the fires breaking out again in India and Pakistan, in Vietnam, in the Middle East, in Northern Ireland, in Latin America, in Africa. These are children murdering children, but we are all to blame. Violence breeds violence. I will save you from yourselves, children of men. Biologically, scientifically I will bring you salvation. Hear my words. Eradicate your violent tendencies or I will operate on your brains. . .

HAWORTH. *(Picking up her chair and advancing on* PONDEN) I'm going to bash your head in.

PONDEN. Childish fantasy.

HAWORTH. Take the consequences. *(Throws chair at* PONDEN)

PONDEN. *(Catching chair)* I'm a white male liberal and you can't frighten me.

HAWORTH. *(Picking up* HEBDEN's *chair and advancing on* PONDEN) Fat suburban slob.

PONDEN. *(Wielding chair)* Come on and try it, baby-face.

HAWORTH. *(Attacking him with chair)* Take that for your power-structure.

PONDEN. *(Parrying attack)* I don't believe in violence.

HEBDEN. *(Joining fight with third chair)* Break it up, children.

PONDEN. I don't believe in violence, but I will not be intimidated.

HAWORTH. I'm fighting for the Vietcong, the American Indians, the Czechoslovakians, the Welsh Nationalists, the Black Africans, the Black Americans, and all oppressed peoples of the world.

PONDEN. I'm not against any of those people. I'm looking for a peaceful solution to the world's problems.

(They are now battling furiously with their chairs)

16

HEBDEN.   Break it up now. You'll do yourselves an
   injury.

HAWORTH.   I'm fighting for the Irish Catholics.

PONDEN.   I'm not against the Irish Catholics, only the
   IRA gunmen.

HAWORTH.   Down with Enoch Powell and General Franco.

PONDEN.   I'm against Enoch Powell and General Franco,
   but not by violent means.

HAWORTH.   What about Ian Smith and the Rhodesian Front?

PONDEN.   Out with them, but no violence.

HEBDEN.   Vorster and the Berlin Wall.

HAWORTH.   Out, out!

HEBDEN.   Nixon and the Brazilian torturers.

HAWORTH.   Out, out!

   (PONDEN *is retreating before the combined attack
   of* HEBDEN *and* HAWORTH)

KEIGHLEY.   *(Sitting up suddenly)* What about the Greek
   Colonels?

PONDEN.   Everybody's against the Greek Colonels.

   (The three of them close round KEIGHLEY, *their
   chairs lifted over their heads. They pause for a
   moment in this position, then replace their chairs
   to make the car and sit down.* PONDEN *and*
   HAWORTH *move their arms like windscreen
   wipers.)*

KEIGHLEY.   Did I say something?

HAWORTH.   You were asleep.

HEBDEN.   Your head was knocking against the window.

KEIGHLEY.   There's a smell of burning.

PONDEN.   *(Sniffing)* Yes. Could it be the wipers?

   (He and HAWORTH *stop moving their arms)*

HEBDEN.   That's the end of the rain. Blue sky ahead.

KEIGHLEY.   *(Looking out of his 'window')* It's
   heading south. Look at them, black clouds making
   for London like waves of German bombers. People
   in Watford are starting to open their umbrellas,
   anxious faces in Harrow are raised like white

17

crocuses to the sky, Edgware has felt the first splash, shoppers in Barnet are scurrying for shelter.

PONDEN. *(Putting left arm round* HAWORTH's *shoulders)* We're really tremendously fond of one another.

HAWORTH. Speak for yourself.

PONDEN. Why does she live with me if she's not fond of me?

(Pause)

HEBDEN. Why does she?

HAWORTH. I couldn't stand living with somebody ugly.

PONDEN. Yes, I am a handsome fellow.

HAWORTH. You're less ugly than some.

HEBDEN. Any other reason?

HAWORTH. He's not rich, but he has a steady income.

HEBDEN. Anything else?

HAWORTH. I don't think so.

HEBDEN. Suppose you fell in with somebody much better-looking and much richer? Richard Burton, for instance, or the Shah of Persia?

HAWORTH. It would depend whether he was a deadly dull person.

HEBDEN. Is this one dull?

HAWORTH. He's not what you'd call exciting.

HEBDEN. *(To* PONDEN) What about you?

PONDEN. I have a fondness for her. She has faults, of of course. Venial faults, it's true, but they make up in quantity what they lack in quality. All the same, I have a fondness for her. I'm supposed to be a professional critic with a well-formed taste, but I'll even admit to a secret affection for the absolutely dreadful novels she writes.

(HAWORTH *pounds* PONDEN *with her fists)*

Look out, we'll have a spill. *(She continues to pound him)* Hold her off, for God's sake, or

there'll be a nasty accident. I'm not insured for
hitch-hikers.

(HEBDEN *struggles with* HAWORTH)

HAWORTH.   Let me out, let me out, let me out!

PONDEN.   What do you want to get out for? We're in
the middle of nowhere.

HAWORTH.   Let me out, or I'll bloody well break the
window.

PONDEN.   If you insist. Wait till I pull on to the hard
shoulder. It's all yours, Nottinghamshire to your
right, Derbyshire to your left.

(HAWORTH *runs off behind curtains up-stage.*
PONDEN *and* HEBDEN *stand near the chairs*)

HEBDEN.   What's she going to do?

PONDEN.   Who knows?

HEBDEN.   She's running across that ploughed field.

PONDEN.   Perhaps that will tire her out.

HEBDEN.   What are you going to do?

PONDEN.   Wait.

HEBDEN.   And if she doesn't come back?

PONDEN.   Women can be awfully annoying, can't they?
Always play games to the bitter end.

HEBDEN.   You ought to beat her. She'd respect you for
it.

PONDEN.   Yes, I'm afraid she would.

(They stand in front of curtains. KEIGHLEY's *head
drops in sleep)*

HEBDEN.   His head's knocking on the window.

PONDEN.   Open it, then.

HEBDEN.   I can't open it. The hasp has rusted.

PONDEN.   Smash the glass.

HEBDEN.   How?

PONDEN.   Put your fist through it.

(HEBDEN *plunges his arm through the curtains)*

HAWORTH.   *(Behind curtain)* Let me in, let me in.

19

PONDEN. Who's that?

HAWORTH. I've come home. I lost my way in the ploughed field.

HEBDEN. It's a child. A horrible white-faced child. I can see its face out there in the darkness like a crocus.

PONDEN. Don't let it in.

HEBDEN. It's grabbed hold of my hand.

HAWORTH. Let me in.

PONDEN. Leave this to me. Stand aside.

HEBDEN. How can I? It won't let go of my hand.

PONDEN. *(Taking* HEBDEN *round waist and pulling)* Pull then, pull like the devil.

HEBDEN. It's coming through the window.

PONDEN. Now saw, saw, saw. Saw its wrist on the jagged glass. Go on, rub it to and fro. That's it, rub, rub, rub!

(They move HEBDEN's *arm to and fro behind the curtain)*

HAWORTH. Let me in.

PONDEN. Never let her in. Never let her in. Never.

(KEIGHLEY *half wakes.* PONDEN *and* HEBDEN *tumble backwards and lie in a heap,* HEBDEN's *arm stretched in the air, his hand bloody.* KEIGHLEY *sits up and opens his eyes)*

KEIGHLEY. Why are you so cruel?

(PONDEN *and* HEBDEN *come and stand near* KEIGHLEY)

HEBDEN. She's vanished over the sky-line. I got this for my trouble.

(He binds up his hand with a handkerchief)

KEIGHLEY. You ought to wash it first.

HEBDEN. It's only barbed wire. Fresh wire, not rusty. Nothing serious.

PONDEN. Damn! Here come the police. Always when they're least wanted.

HEBDEN. They'll move you on.

PONDEN. I'll tell them what happend.

HEBDEN. They won't believe you, it's not a very
likely story.

PONDEN. *(Laughing)* Quite funny, though.

KEIGHLEY. Don't laugh. The fuzz don't like people
who laugh.

PONDEN. We'll have to just drive on and leave her,
hot-footing it in the general direction of Liverpool.

(HEBDEN *and* PONDEN *laugh. They put their
arms on one another's shoulders and laugh together,
while* KEIGHLEY *looks on with a serious face)*

TAPE. Authors are supposed to love their characters.
Do I love my shades? Yes, as a cat loves a mouse,
as a hawk an escaped canary, as a blackbird a
wriggling worm. They promise me an hour or so's
amusement. I shall treat myself to a slow vivisection
of these helpless ninnies.

6. POTATOES, A DOG AND MRS HICKS

(PONDEN *turns one chair to face up-stage, sits and
writes in notebook on knee.* KEIGHLEY *sits facing
audience, his feet on another chair.* HEBDEN *off left,*
HAWORTH *behind curtains)*

HEBDEN. *(Off)* Come and peel the potatoes.

(KEIGHLEY *gets up, goes off up-left, returns with
saucepan and bag of potatoes. He peels potatoes
and puts them in pan)*

PONDEN. *(Not looking round)* What's he so busy with?

KEIGHLEY. Skinning those rabbits.

PONDEN. I admire his competence in the kitchen.

KEIGHLEY. He was in prison.

PONDEN. Was he? I'd never have guessed.

KEIGHLEY. That's where he learnt to cater.

(HEBDEN *enters, wearing cook's apron smeared
with blood, a bloody knife in one hand, dustpan
and brush in the other)*

HEBDEN. *(To* KEIGHLEY) Take your feet off that
chair.

(KEIGHLEY *does so*)

(To PONDEN) Are you making yourself useful?

PONDEN.   Hardly in a practical sense. I'm jotting down notes for my lecture.

HEBDEN.   Someone's left fids of mud on the carpet. *(Gives* PONDEN *dustpan and brush and goes out left)*

PONDEN.   *(On hands and knees, sweeping floor)* This house is much better run since you moved in. Why was he in prison?

KEIGHLEY.   He killed a dog.

PONDEN.   How unfortunate! Ran over it?

KEIGHLEY.   Hit it between the eyes with his fist.

PONDEN.   No!

KEIGHLEY.   Didn't mean to kill it. He was very fond of that dog.

PONDEN.   His own dog, was it?

KEIGHLEY.   It was a big dog, Alsatian or partly. But he didn't like it sleeping on the bed. He dragged it downstairs by the collar, it was growling angrily, and at the bottom of the stairs by the broom-cupboard he let it go. He was going to beat it with a stick from the hall-stand but there wasn't time. Its eyes were shining in the darkness under the stairs and it was growling louder and louder. Suddenly it leapt at his throat and he hit it. Right between the eyes with his fist.

PONDEN.   Good gracious!

KEIGHLEY.   The magistrate said he deserved to hang. The dog would have understood. The dog was very fond of him. The dog wouldn't have wanted him to go to prison.

(Pause, then tapping sound on window behind curtains)

PONDEN.   What's that? *(He gets up and peers between curtains)*

KEIGHLEY.   What is it?

PONDEN.   I'm trying to see.

22

HAWORTH. *(Outside)* Let me in.

KEIGHLEY. It's her.

PONDEN. I believe it is.

> *(He helps* HAWORTH *through curtains)*
>
> You've come home. We'd given you up for lost.
>
> (HAWORTH *sits on chair. She is giggling hysterically)*

KEIGHLEY. You're soaking wet. Look at her clothes, she's all over mud.

HAWORTH. *(Giggling)* I've come home.

PONDEN. The police moved us on. They didn't believe our story about losing you.

HAWORTH. They must have had second thoughts. When I came back to the motorway, there were policemen everywhere, dragging the ditches, poking about in copses and spinneys, consulting transistor radios and wearing wellington boots.

> *(Enter* HEBDEN *with bloody hands)*

HEBDEN. Take off your clothes. It's madness to sit about in that state. I'll get some hot water.

> *(He goes out)*

PONDEN. Better do what he says.

> (PONDEN *and* KEIGHLEY *help* HAWORTH *off with her clothes)*

HAWORTH. They took me to the nearest railway station. They were very fatherly. They even gave me money for the fare.

> (HEBDEN *enters with steaming bowl of water, towel and dressing-gown. He puts* HAWORTH's *feet in water and helps her to put on dressing-gown)*

PONDEN. But that was three months ago. Why did it take you so long to get here?

HAWORTH. I had a job at the railway-station.

HEBDEN. *(Massaging* HAWORTH's *feet and legs in the water)* How did you get in such a state?

HAWORTH. I was running away.

PONDEN. What on earth induced you to take a job at the railway-station?

HAWORTH. They were short of a booking-clerk.

HEBDEN. Why were you running away?

HAWORTH. That was later.

PONDEN. You might have let us know you were all right. We were worried about you.

HAWORTH. I wasn't all right. I was treated very badly.

HEBDEN. Who treated you badly?

HAWORTH. My husband.

(All freeze in positions of astonishment)

I married the porter at the railway-station. He used to beat me every night.

PONDEN. Why?

HAWORTH. My bad cooking. At first I didn't mind, I found him so attractive. But then I stopped finding him attractive and he went on beating me and it all seemed too much, so I ran away.

KEIGHLEY. On foot?

HAWORTH. Yes. He always took my money.

PONDEN. Does he know you've run away?

HAWORTH. He tried to stop me. Look. *(Turns her head and pushes forward one ear)* It's bleeding again now with the warmth of the room.

PONDEN. How awful!

HAWORTH. He threw a table-knife at me as I ran out of the back door which for once he'd forgotten to lock. But that's nothing to what he said he'd do. As I was climbing the garden fence he said he could see my white face in the dark and if he ever caught me he was going to paint it all the colours of the rainbow.

KEIGHLEY. Did he give chase?

HAWORTH. He was too drunk. He fell over the foot-scraper outside the back door.

HEBDEN. I'll fetch some Dettol for that wound behind your ear.

(HEBDEN *goes out with bowl of water)*

KEIGHLEY. I'll get you some slippers.

(KEIGHLEY *goes out with towel and* HAWORTH's *cast-off clothes)*

PONDEN. What an adventure! So you're a married woman now?

HAWORTH. It will make a difference, won't it?

PONDEN. I suppose it will.

HAWORTH. We shall be adulterers.

PONDEN. Yes, I see.

HAWORTH. More exciting in every way. Give me a kiss now and see what it feels like.

(They kiss. HEBDEN *and* KEIGHLEY *are standing at the edge of the stage watching)*

HAWORTH. What do you think? Doesn't it add an extra something?

PONDEN. What's your name now? Your new name?

HAWORTH. Hicks. Mrs. Hicks.

PONDEN. Mrs. Hicks, I have a great fondness for you. *(They kiss)*

TAPE. Is there nothing I can do to bring home to them the sheer misery of their situation? Everything I do to them only makes them secrete a sort of slime of domesticity and acceptance. Do they imagine that what they suffer comes about by chance? Are they not aware that they are the playthings of a vicious and malevolent creator? Desperate measures are called for.

7. A VIEW OF WUTHERING HEIGHTS

(PONDEN *sits on chair facing up-stage as before, with notebook and pen on knee.* HAWORTH *sits facing audience and looking into space.* KEIGHLEY, *sitting near her, knits a baby's coat)*

HAWORTH. What shall we do now?

PONDEN. Why don't you go to bed?

HAWORTH. Anything but that. Haven't you finished your lecture?

PONDEN. Very nearly.

KEIGHLEY. What's it about this week?

PONDEN. *(Turning round)* This week I'm tackling a
very difficult work by the nineteenth-century
novelist Emily Brontë. My view is this: the theme
of *Wuthering Heights* is not the clash between good
and evil, as some have supposed, but between the
human and the inhuman. By the inhuman I don't
mean simply cruelty and violence, but everything
which is not specifically human. Nature is
inhuman—rocks, rivers, moors, rain, storm, snow,
sun, and so forth. Animals are inhuman. But the
really interesting point is that human beings
themselves contain large elements of the inhuman,
and these are the elements which they share with
the rest of the natural world. Again, I don't mean
simply the bad parts of our nature. I would
consider sexual attraction between human beings
as an inhuman or natural element in this sense;
the instinctive love of a mother for her child is
essentially inhuman; physical pain and pleasure are
inhuman, so are possessiveness, fear, anger and so
on. When I say human I mean those elements which
are *only* found in human beings, such as pity,
mercy, rationality, and less attractive qualities
such as fraud, and ideological or religious fanaticism.
Everything man-made is also human—cities are
human, roads, books, bulldozers; guns are human,
gas-chambers are human, money is human. You
see what I'm getting at?

(Enter HEBDEN *with three cups of tea and glass
of milk)*

Cups of tea are human.

HAWORTH. But milk is inhuman. Why do I have to
have milk?

HEBDEN. Milk is what you need in your inhuman
condition.

PONDEN. Now it's just at this stage in our history that
the human is beginning to dominate the inhuman.
The natural world is in full retreat. The importance
of Emily Brontë's novel, as I see it, is that it was
written at the turning-point, at the moment when
the human and the inhuman were more or less in

26

balance. And Emily Brontë seems to have felt an equal attraction to both. The strength of her book is that she doesn't take sides.

HEBDEN. But aren't you on the human side?

PONDEN. I suppose that by and large I am. I don't entirely approve of *Wuthering Heights,* you know, but I can't help admiring and feeling its force.

(He returns to scribbling in his notebook. HAWORTH stares into space. KEIGHLEY puts down his knitting and stares into space. HEBDEN stares into his cup of tea)

8. THE GODS DISPOSE

(All four actors sitting as in previous scene)

HAWORTH. I don't know what to do.

HEBDEN. Nor do I.

KEIGHLEY. Nor do I.

PONDEN. Why not go to bed?

HAWORTH. Anything but that.

(Silence, while they sip tea. Then PONDEN raises head)

PONDEN. Suppose we each had an island of our own. A small island.

HAWORTH. Cuba?

PONDEN. If you like. I thought you'd choose Cuba. I'd choose the Isle of Wight.

HEBDEN. Why?

PONDEN. I read somewhere that there's still standing-room on the Isle of Wight for the whole population of the globe.

HEBDEN. I'd take Samoa or Tahiti.

HAWORTH. Why?

HEBDEN. Samoa for Robert Louis Stevenson, Tahiti for Gauguin. Places to escape to.

KEIGHLEY. Guernsey.

HAWORTH. Why on earth Guernsey?

27

KEIGHLEY. I like the cows.

PONDEN. And who would you have as top men in your islands?

HEBDEN. Living or dead?

PONDEN. Living.

HAWORTH. I'd have Fidel Castro, Herbert Marcuse and Stokely Carmichael.

HEBDEN. Lévi-Strauss, Samuel Beckett and Pablo Neruda.

KEIGHLEY. Trevor Huddleston, Father Vicini, General Grigorenko.

PONDEN. Mine would be Alexander Dubcek, General Dayan and Willy Brandt.

(They smile at one another, sipping their tea)

PONDEN. Now this floor is the world—the whole earth's surface. We need some figures.

HAWORTH. The toy-soldiers.

PONDEN. Yes.

(HAWORTH *goes off. The others move the chairs back to the edges of the stage and take the cups away.* HAWORTH *returns with four wooden soldiers, each a foot or so high)*

PONDEN. Yes. *(Takes one of the soldiers)* This is Alexander Dubcek. This fine, upstanding, courageous, liberal toy-soldier will be Alexander Dubcek.

HEBDEN. *(Taking soldier)* This is mine. Samuel Barclay Beckett.

KEIGHLEY. *(Taking soldier)* This is my bishop. Trevor Huddleston.

HAWORTH. *(Holding up fourth soldier)* I've changed my mind about Fidel Castro. Mine is the revolutionary hero Che Guevara.

PONDEN. Che Guevara's dead.

HAWORTH. Who says so? I don't believe he's dead.

PONDEN. Have it your own way. We'll put our leaders on their islands now. *(Puts his soldier up left*

28

centre) Dubcek on the Isle of Wight.

HAWORTH. *(Putting her soldier down right of*
PONDEN's) Che Guevara returns to Cuba.

KEIGHLEY. *(Putting soldier down left of*
PONDEN's) Trevor Huddleston, President of
Guernsey.

HEBDEN. *(Putting soldier right of* HAWORTH's)
Samuel Beckett on Samoa.

PONDEN. This floor, the world, is a seething maelstrom
of horror and misery, of wars, poverty, crime,
frustration and suffering. But on these four small
islands matters should soon begin to improve. We
are the gods and we have picked out four just men
to solve the problems of humanity and demonstrate
the virtues of peace and good government.

HEBDEN. Suppose they make a mess of it?

(PONDEN *takes* HAWORTH's *hand with his right,*
KEIGHLEY's *with his left.* HAWORTH *takes*
HEBDEN's *hand with her right. They stand*
behind the four soldiers, their linked arms raised)

PONDEN. The gods solemnly declare that unless the
four just men—namely Alexander Dubcek, Che
Guevara, Samuel Beckett and Trevor Huddleston—
succeed in solving the problems of humanity, the
earth will be laid waste for ever.

(The four walk solemnly round the soldiers)

ALL. This is the last time and this we all agree.

HAWORTH. *(Standing in the centre while the others*
circle) Wars, tidal waves, droughts and hurricanes
will reduce every land to a desert.

KEIGHLEY. *(Taking her place in the centre)* Rivers,
streams, lakes and seas will be polluted with
noxious substances and nauseous vapours.

PONDEN. *(Taking* KEIGHLEY's *place at centre)*
Those living creatures that remain will be torn to
pieces by mushroom explosions, seared by white-
hot blasts and hideously mutilated by whirlwinds
of radio-active dust.

HEBDEN. *(Taking* PONDEN's *place at centre)* The
world will be engulfed in flames and poisonous
gases. When every trace of life has been obliterated,

29

this barren ball of fissured rock and stagnant water
will plunge out of its customary orbit and roll away
through the vast wilderness of space like a dislodged
boulder, crashing into moons and planets, wreaking
havoc on the whole solar system, displacing other
heavenly bodies and causing them to shoot
furiously through the universe, breaking up the
intricate patterns of the constellations, exploding
distant stars, reducing the infinite and ineffable
order of the cosmos to a single pitchy mass of
chaos.

(All four circle the soldiers again)

ALL. This is the last time and this we all agree.

*(They stand on the chairs round the edges of the
stage)*

PONDEN. Alexander Dubcek. . .

(They clap their hands)

HEBDEN. Samuel Beckett. . .

(They clap their hands)

HAWORTH. Che Guevara. . .

(They clap their hands)

KEIGHLEY. Trevor Huddleston. . .

(They clap their hands)

PONDEN. Do your stuff.

ALL. Do your stuff.

PONDEN. We are watching you.

ALL. We are watching you.

*(They squat on their chairs, looking earnestly at
the toy-soldiers, then get down and return chairs
to positions of last scene)*

9. HICKS

(HEBDEN *removes toy-soldiers.* KEIGHLEY
removes cups of tea. HAWORTH *and* PONDEN
sit on chairs as in scene 7. HEBDEN *stands on
chair at edge of stage)*

KEIGHLEY. A person from the railway-station wishes
to see you.

30

TAPE. No, I'm not introducing another shade. This is to be a personal intervention. Somebody's going to get hurt, I'll see to that myself.

(KEIGHLEY *goes to edge of stage and picks up tambourine*)

PONDEN. *(Rising, putting hand on chair-back and confronting his visitor firmly with legs apart)* Come in, come in.

(HAWORTH *retreats to far corner of stage,* PONDEN *looks up at the invisible intruder, who is perhaps five or six times his own height)*

PONDEN. Mr. Hicks, I presume?

HEBDEN. Big fellow, big and black. Huge.

(KEIGHLEY *rattles tambourine*)

PONDEN. What can I do for you, Mr. Hicks?

(KEIGHLEY *hits tambourine, simultaneously* PONDEN *staggers back with hand to side of his face)*

HEBDEN. Hicks has sloshed him.

PONDEN. Not a very friendly action, Mr. Hicks. I had word you were a violent sort of man and you've not failed to live up to your reputation. However, I am not a violent man and I do not propose to return your blow. On the contrary. . .

(PONDEN *advances with a certain hesitancy and inclines the other side of his head towards the intruder)*

HEBDEN. Our man's offering Hicks the other cheek.

(KEIGHLEY *bangs tambourine.* PONDEN *staggers back with hand to other side of his head)*

HEBDEN. Hicks has sloshed him again.

PONDEN. I refuse to be provoked, Mr. Hicks.

HAWORTH. *(Still cowering in her corner)* Oh, for God's sake, don't be such a rabbit. He doesn't have a brain, so it's no good reasoning with him.

PONDEN. Allow me to handle this in my own way. *(Standing beside chair, as KEIGHLEY rattles tambourine)* Here is a chair, my dear chap, why don't you take a seat and we can discuss the whole affair in a civilized manner?

(KEIGHLEY *hits tambourine.* PONDEN *clutches his stomach and falls over the chair)*

HEBDEN.   Hicks has socked him in the solar plexus. Our man's resting on the ropes.

PONDEN.   *(Breathing painfully)* Mr. Hicks, you are behaving like a mere brute.

HAWORTH.   He is a brute, you silly goof. I told you, there's nothing behind those bloodshot eyes.

(KEIGHLEY *hits tambourine twice in quick succession.* HAWORTH *clutches head and falls to the ground)*

HEBDEN.   Now she's down and Hicks is kicking her.

(KEIGHLEY *hits tambourine four times)*

Two...three...four...

HAWORTH.   Why don't you do something? *(Writhing on ground and curling into a ball)*

PONDEN.   *(Getting to his feet and advancing shakily a few steps, while* KEIGHLEY *rattles tambourine)* Unless you leave this house immediately, Mr. Hicks, I shall call the police.

(KEIGHLEY *hits tambourine.* PONDEN *dives backwards and lies spreadeagled on floor)*

HEBDEN.   Our man's on the floor.

PONDEN.   *(Rising again, to rattle of tambourine)* Enough is enough, Mr. Hicks. You can push a man so far, but no further. I am not a barbarian, but neither am I a coward. *(Punching the air wildly he moves forward)*

(KEIGHLEY *hits tambourine,* PONDEN *goes down on his face.* KEIGHLEY *rattles tambourine, as* PONDEN *and* HAWORTH *appear to be lifted to their feet by the scruff of their necks, then rushed together across the stage.* KEIGHLEY *hits tambourine as they meet centre stage, then rattles it as they stagger apart again, hits it as they meet, rattles as they part, hits it for the last time, as they meet and sink down together centre stage)*

HEBDEN.   Hicks is administering the double bounce

and *coup de grâce.*

(HAWORTH *and* PONDEN *lie still on the stage.*
KEIGHLEY *comes out and stands near them)*

KEIGHLEY. Mr. Hicks has gone.

PONDEN. That fellow ought to be locked up.

HAWORTH. Why don't you ring the police? Or maybe
the army?

(HEBDEN *comes down from his chair)*

HEBDEN. I'll make a fresh pot of tea.

TAPE. Effective so far as it goes. But crude. Let us try
something more subtly damaging than physical
violence.

10. THE BABY

(KEIGHLEY *sets step-ladder up-right, with bundle on
top step. HAWORTH sits on chair centre, knitting
something for her baby. KEIGHLEY sits on chair right of
her, not far from step-ladder. PONDEN off left.
HEBDEN enters from up-left with cups of tea)*

HEBDEN. Baby's crying.

HAWORTH. Yes, I heard it too. Mothers have specially
sensitive hearing, I believe.

HEBDEN. You don't need sensitive hearing for this
one. He's yelling his insides out.

HAWORTH. It's best to let them cry a bit, it's supposed
to be good for them.

HEBDEN. Nonsense! Just listen to him. Do you think
that's good for him?

KEIGHLEY. Why is it supposed to be good for him?

HAWORTH. I've no idea. I daresay it develops the
lungs, or expands the blood-vessels.

HEBDEN. Bloody nonsense! I'll bet it does him untold
harm psychologically.

HAWORTH. Rubbish.

HEBDEN. In later life that child will turn into some
sort of pervert, mark my words.

(They sip their tea in silence)

33

KEIGHLEY. Aren't you going to give him a name?

HAWORTH. Eventually.

HEBDEN. What about Caspar? That's a name I like.

HAWORTH. I can't give him a name until I've made up my mind whose child he is.

HEBDEN. There's no doubt whose child he is. Look at the colour of his hair.

HAWORTH. That proves nothing. He has a definite look of Hicks.

KEIGHLEY. He's got small eyes.

HEBDEN. But he hasn't got Hicks's colouring. If he was the son of Hicks, he'd be a whole lot swarthier.

KEIGHLEY. He's still shouting.

HEBDEN. I'll go and talk to him.

HAWORTH. Leave him alone. I'll go up in a minute.

(They freeze. PONDEN *comes on stage down left. He is carrying a briefcase.* KEIGHLEY *puts down tea-cup and goes to meet him.* HEBDEN *and* HAWORTH *remain in freeze positions)*

PONDEN. Sorry I'm late. So many questions. Not like last year's lecture, must be a brighter crowd of students this year. One question in particular struck me as very shrewd. Did I count birth — the act of birth — as inhuman or human? Definitely inhuman, I said, unless we start producing babies out of test-tubes. Then what about death, he said. Ah death, I said. No doubt on that score. Inhuman every time. Well then, said my interrogator, how is it you claim the human is already in a dominant position over the inhuman, when there's death? You're absolutely right, I said, until we abolish death, the natural world has got us by the short hairs every time. So your whole thesis goes out of the window, he said, and the room was hushed, waiting to see how I'd get out of that one. We may say if we like, I replied, that the inhuman *ultimately* dominates the human, as the universe dominates the earth; but within the confines of our life (which is time as we know it) and our world (which is space as we know it) the human is now unquestionably the dominant factor. Was

34

that well returned or wasn't it?

KEIGHLEY.   It was nobody's fault. Please understand that. Not his, not hers, not mine. All the same it should never have happened.

(PONDEN *freezes.* KEIGHLEY *returns to his chair.* HAWORTH *and* HEBDEN *start to move again, sipping their tea)*

HEBDEN.   Did Hicks used to shout much?

HAWORTH.   He hardly ever spoke a word.

HEBDEN.   Well, if this is Hicks's child, it certainly doesn't take after him in that.

HAWORTH.   I'll go when I've finished my tea.

KEIGHLEY.   The baby's other father talks all the time.

HEBDEN.   Right. I wouldn't be surprised if this baby grew up to be some sort of lecturer.

KEIGHLEY.   He's reaching a climax.

HAWORTH.   I'm going.

HEBDEN.   Let me go. I'm on my feet. I'll bring him down.

(HEBDEN *puts down tea-cup, goes right and mounts steps. At the top of the steps he picks up bundle, turns round and comes down a step or two)*

HEBDEN.   *(Holding up bundle)* Here he is. Red in the face, but quite happy now. He was getting lonely up there. Weren't you, Caspar, weren't you getting lonely?

HAWORTH.   His name is not Caspar.

HEBDEN.   *(To bundle)* What are we going to call you, then? Who's your father, boy?

HAWORTH.   If anything's going to give him problems, it's asking him questions like that.

HEBDEN.   He's decided to have me. He's decided I'm the kindest father on the premises. Haven't you, boy? You like a bit of a bounce, don't you? Bounce, bounce, bounce. *(Bouncing the bundle)* He's laughing all over his face. No, you certainly don't look like Hicks, do you? But you don't care who your father is, all you want is a bit of a

35

bounce. (He throws bundle up gently and catches it) Up. . .down.Up. . .down. Up. . .Christ!

(As HEBDEN *seems to drop bundle downstage of steps,* KEIGHLEY *leaps up and stretches out one hand towards it.* HAWORTH *leans forward on her chair, watching. The bundle rests between* HEBDEN's *outstretched left hand and* KEIGHLEY's *outstretched right. They freeze in these positions, while tape plays)*

TAPE.   Shall I save it or shan't I? In a manner of speaking it's my own child, shade of my shades. Sentimentality! I only brought it into being from malice — to hurt them. To them it's a living child, to me it's nothing but a stage-prop.

(HEBDEN *and* KEIGHLEY *let the bundle drop to the floor.* HAWORTH *rises from her chair.* KEIGHLEY *kneels on floor near bundle.* HEBDEN *looks down)*

TAPE.   I have no pity. The more the worms writhe, the more I yearn to crush out their entrails. It's a moral teething, and I grind with greater energy the more I increase their pain.

(HAWORTH *sits on chair, takes up knitting.* HEBDEN *comes down and stands by steps.* KEIGHLEY *crosses to* PONDEN)

KEIGHLEY.   There was nothing we could do. It was lying in that dark corner by the broom-cupboard.

PONDEN.   Where are the others?

KEIGHLEY.   He's outside. She's still sitting in her chair.

11. THE LIGHTNING CONDUCTOR

(PONDEN *kneels beside* HAWORTH, *still sitting in her chair. They remain like this throughout the scene.* HEBDEN *stands beside steps,* KEIGHLEY *facing him from down right)*

KEIGHLEY.   You've been here all night and you've not budged an inch. There's a pair of ousels making a nest in the tree over your head and they've stopped bothering about you. They only flew away when they saw me coming. I can tell you haven't stirred all night, because there's only one pair of footprints coming across the heavy dew on the lawn, and those are mine.

HEBDEN.   I'm warning you. Don't come too close.

KEIGHLEY.   I'm not afraid of you.

HEBDEN.   I'm not a harmless person. I may look like a harmless person, innocent people may form the impression that I am a harmless person, but magistrates with their wits about them know better.

KEIGHLEY.   Everybody knows it wasn't your fault.

HEBDEN.   Harmless people do not throw cups of hot tea in other people's faces. I've no right to go about deceiving people. They look at me, all the harmless people, just a glance out of the corner of the eye in the normal way to check up -- who's this fellow next to me in the queue? — and say to themselves, all's well, don't worry, he's got a nose, two eyes, two ears and a mouth in the correct places, he's of average human height and all four limbs appear to be in working order, he is not green in the face, his ears are not pointed, his hair grows naturally, he has no tail; nor is he covered in scabs or scales, he's breathing regularly, he sees, he hears, he even speaks, he's one of us, and they look away again as if they had nothing to fear. Should I wear something in my lapel, then? Should I carry a placard THIS ANIMAL BITES or ring a little bell UNCLEAN, UNCLEAN, should I say to them in a hoarse voice, stand further off, keep your distance, I am not as safe as I look, don't tangle with me if you value your life or your loved ones?

KEIGHLEY.   Come inside.

HEBDEN.   You must be out of your mind. Lightning never strikes twice in the same place: is that your view? But it strikes a lightning conductor, yes it does, once, twice, three times, four, five, again and again. The purpose of lightning conductors after all is to carry lethal electric charges harmlessly into the earth. You don't ask lightning conductors to make friends with dogs, or take rides in your car, or mind the baby. You put them on chimney-stacks, and in the tops of tall trees, you don't invite them into your house, you don't offer them cups of tea.

(HEBDEN *and* KEIGHLEY *remain in these positions for a moment or two, then go behind curtains*)

12. THE BALL OF WOOL

(PONDEN *kneeling beside* HAWORTH. *She unwinds her piece of knitting and rolls the wool into a ball*)

HAWORTH.   When I was small, I had a passion for balls of wool, especially their colours. I couldn't bear people to make use of them, to knit them officiously into garments, useful garments. Even the colours were spoilt when you knew they were meant to wear. That's what I most disliked about grown-up people, the way they couldn't be content with balls of wool, with things that were perfect in themselves and self-contained, but had to be turning them into an object which Auntie This or That would recognise with tweets of delight — a coatee or a bootee or a stupid little cap with a bobble on it. And then I grew up myself and this compulsion came over me to make something recognisable, to turn this perfectly pointless object into something else, something with a pattern and a purpose. I think I shall break with all that, I should like to go back to being small.

(Pause)

There are three people outside the window.

PONDEN.   There's nothing outside the window.

HAWORTH.   There are three people looking in.

PONDEN.   Nonsense. The curtains are closed, nobody can look in.

HAWORTH.   There are three women outside the window looking in. Their faces are shining in the dark.

PONDEN.   I promise you, you're wrong.

HAWORTH.   The women have all been dead for more than a hundred years, but they're looking in and their faces are shining.

PONDEN.   Turn round and see. *(He turns her chair to face curtains)* Look, the curtains are closed, there's nobody there.

HAWORTH. They're just outside the window. Tell them to go away.

PONDEN. I promise you. . .

HAWORTH. Go out and drive them away.

PONDEN. Really, it's nonsense. . .

HAWORTH. Drive them away!

PONDEN. All right, I'll do that, but promise you won't think about them again if I do that for you.

(He gets up)

I'll drive them away and I'll be back at once. Will you be all right?

(Pause, then PONDEN *goes behind curtains)*

PONDEN. *(From outside window)* There's no one here.

(The curtains open. Light shines on the painting with the three actors' faces showing through the holes as in the opening scene. HAWORTH sits still in her chair staring at painting. On the tape, the sound of a powerful car accelerating and fading into the distance)

PART TWO

WUTHERING HEIGHTS

13. THE GODS REPORT

(The four actors enter and place their toy-soldiers on the floor, in the same positions as before. Then they go and stand on their chairs round the edge of the stage)

PONDEN.   After a suitable lapse of time, the gods meet again to consider the fate of the world. The business of the day is to hear interim reports on the conduct of the four just men.

HAWORTH.   *(Getting down from chair and standing beside her toy-soldier)* Bad news from Cuba. Looking down at this moment I can see Che Guevara resting against the bole of a tree in the Sierra Maestra. He is wounded, his head is bound with a bloody bandage, only a handful of weary comrades are with him. Spotter planes are circling overhead, troops and tanks are drawing the net tighter around his hiding-place.

PONDEN.   Very grave, very grave. But how did he get into such a tight spot?

HAWORTH.   It was the North Americans. Hearing that Che was not dead, hearing he had returned to Cuba, they panicked. In a moment of weakness, bullied by his generals, the President signed an order. Immediately contingency plans were put into effect. Armed Cuban exiles, supplemented by several divisions of 'volunteers', launched a full-scale attack by air and sea. Marines landed at chosen points round the coast, paratroops descended like poisonous mushrooms, nuclear submarines ringed the island. Havana was ablaze from end to end when at last Che gave the order to evacuate. I myself stood on the war-shaken shores of Cuba; I myself saw flames consume the sugar-harvest; I myself saw the defiled and violated city of Havana, its lurid reflections in the sea, its broken and blackened windows from which the barbaric faces of the invader looked out.

(HAWORTH *returns to her chair.* PONDEN *gets down from his and stands beside his toy-soldier)*

41

PONDEN.   Alexander Dubcek has been more fortunate on the Isle of Wight. Having first established a system of equal education, equal pay and equal social status for all the inhabitants, he has succeeded in eradicating poverty and crime. He has dismantled the police force. Menial tasks are either performed by machines or shared equally amongst the whole population, including intellectuals and members of the government. There is free housing, a free health service and all leisure activities—arts, sports, recreations of every kind—are free. The people work a twelve-hour week, but they are so physically fit, so mentally cultivated and so inwardly contented that the sale of television sets has declined sharply and only a few of the older citizens still watch the programmes. Private cars are unknown. People either travel by public transport, which is all-electric, spotlessly clean and consistently efficient, or else they walk. Due to the fitness of the inhabitants, the average walking-pace in the Isle of Wight is estimated to have risen to six or seven miles an hour. There are problems, of course, the chief being that the immigration laws are very strict, since nearly every visitor to the island wants to stay there permanently.

(PONDEN *returns to his chair.* KEIGHLEY *goes and stands beside his toy-soldier)*

KEIGHLEY.   Trevor Huddleston has thrown open the island of Guernsey to all the refugees in the world, regardless of colour, creed or nationality. Unfortunately the mass exodus of tax-evaders has left the island very poor. Money is no longer used—the currency is milk and tomatoes.

(KEIGHLEY *returns to his chair. Pause)*

PONDEN.   *(To* HEBDEN) And Samuel Beckett?

HEBDEN.   *(Reluctantly going and standing beside his toy-soldier)* There is no news of Samuel Beckett. He is said to be in hiding on the island of Samoa, but the Samoans deny all knowledge of his whereabouts.

(HEBDEN *returns to his chair)*

PONDEN.   Alexander Dubcek. . .

(All clap hands)

HEBDEN.   Samuel Beckett. . .

(All clap hands)

KEIGHLEY. Trevor Huddleston. . .

(All clap hands)

HAWORTH. Che Guevara. . .

(All clap hands)

PONDEN. Keep it up.

ALL. Keep it up.

PONDEN. We are still watching you.

ALL. We are still watching you.

(They get down from their chairs and remove the toy-soldiers)

14. WINDOW-RAPPING

(Positions as in Scene 3: HAWORTH and PONDEN kneeling stage left, looking towards stage right, where HEBDEN and KEIGHLEY are looking through window at them)

TAPE. I tremble with exhilaration. I can hardly hear myself speak. The road is a witches' brew of adverse weather conditions: pelting rain, thunder-claps, stabs of lightning and sheets of spray through which now and again I see the nervous red lights of my fellow-travellers. They are wise enough not to venture into my lane on a night like this. The roar of the engine, the swift beat of the wipers, the fierce hissing of the tyres make a fittingly cacophonous accompaniment to my voice. My shades are now rubbed and chiselled to my will; it only needs a few more turns of the vice to twist them for ever into the grotesque attitudes I have foreseen for them.

HAWORTH. They've come back.

PONDEN. Which is it this time? The three dead women or the two men?

HAWORTH. The two men. The three women come to the other window.

PONDEN. Whichever it is, you mustn't worry. I shan't let them in here.

HAWORTH. How can you keep them out?

PONDEN.   The doors are bolted, the windows are latched.

HAWORTH.   But if they forced their way in?

PONDEN.   My security arrangements are the envy of my insurance company. We're safe as houses.

(HEBDEN *and* KEIGHLEY *make rapping noise stage-right)*

HAWORTH.   They want to come in.

PONDEN.   Of course they want to come in, it's a nasty night outside, but we're not going to let them in, are we?

(KEIGHLEY *and* HEBDEN *walk round front of stage and rap at down-left)*

HAWORTH.   *(Swivelling round in direction of rapping)* There! There! At the front-door.

PONDEN.   Nothing to worry about. Shall I switch on the tele for you?

(KEIGHLEY *and* HEBDEN *go up-left and make rapping noise)*

HAWORTH.   *(Swivelling towards noise)* The back-door now, the back-door!

PONDEN.   Locked and bolted. Would you like me to read to you?

(KEIGHLEY *and* HEBDEN *go behind curtains up-stage and rap.* HAWORTH *swivels to follow noise, but says nothing)*

Yes, now they're at the other window. They're wasting their time, we're snug and cosy, aren't we, and we're not letting them in.

(KEIGHLEY *and* HEBDEN *rap stage-right again. Throughout following* HAWORTH's *head continues to swivel after noise,* PONDEN *watches* HAWORTH)

Round and round, just like clockwork. You wonder they don't get tired of it. Shall I tell you something nice?

(HEBDEN *and* KEIGHLEY, *going faster, rap at stage left, down)*

My salary's being raised this month.

(Rapping at up-left)

So I'm going to buy you a new dress and take you out to that new restaurant for a celebration.

(Rapping behind curtains)

PONDEN.   And in six months' time I expect to be made a professor. . .

(Rapping right)

We'll move to a new house. . .

(KEIGHLEY *and* HEBDEN, *moving still faster, rap down-left)*

Buy a second car. . .

(Rapping at up-left)

Take a long holiday. . .

(Rapping behind curtains)

In Italy perhaps. . .

(Rapping up-right)

Rome of the Caesars. . .

(KEIGHLEY *and* HEBDEN, *going like the clappers, rap down-left)*

Renaissance Florence. . .

(Rapping up-left)

And. . .

(Rapping behind curtains)

Or. . .

(Rapping right)

We'll. . .

(Rapping down-left)

PONDEN.   Won't we?

(Rapping up-left)

We'll. . .

(KEIGHLEY *and* HEBDEN *go off left. Long pause.* HAWORTH *is still staring at curtains waiting for next rap)*

Ah. They've left us in peace at last. Yes. A glass of whisky and time for bed, I should think, wouldn't you?

HAWORTH.   Will you keep your gun under the pillow?

PONDEN.   Of course I will.

HAWORTH.   Your pistol with the spring-knife, in case the bullet misses.

PONDEN.   That's the one. How does the hymn go? *(Sings)* 'Hobgoblin nor foul fiend can daunt his spirit. . .' First the spirit and then to bed. What a lamentable attempt at humour. All right now? All right?

(Putting his arm round her, he leads her out)

15. THE FACE ON THE CRAG

(HEBDEN *puts chairs centre, upside down to represent hearth, then stands beside them. Enter* KEIGHLEY *with haversack)*

HEBDEN.   Come in, come in. He's in a good mood this morning.

KEIGHLEY.   Turned cold again. Snow forecast for tonight.

HEBDEN.   You remembered the oats?

KEIGHLEY.   I got everything you said.

HEBDEN.   He'd fancy a plate of porridge for his breakfast.

KEIGHLEY.   I'll make it. *(Fetches saucepan with a little water in it. Takes packet of oats out of haversack and pours some into saucepan. Mixes result in pan and holds over 'hearth')* What have you been doing this week?

HEBDEN.   Didn't you notice?

KEIGHLEY.   *(Shakes head and stirs)*

HEBDEN.   On your way up?

KEIGHLEY.   No.

HEBDEN.   He's made a portrait of her with two stones, four blades of grass, a snail's shell and a tiny white feather. You want to look at that on your way down.

KEIGHLEY. I will.

HEBDEN. Right at the foot of the signpost where the two paths meet. You wouldn't see it if you weren't looking for it, but he's quite pleased with it.

KEIGHLEY. Haven't you done any work on the crag this week?

HEBDEN. Hasn't he done any work on the crag? He's been up there all hours. Take a look. Go on. Let him stir that and take a look.

(KEIGHLEY *goes to stage-right and looks up*)

Can you see it?

KEIGHLEY. I can see the crag all right.

HEBDEN. And the face?

KEIGHLEY. Can't see any face.

HEBDEN. All week he's been crawling over that crag, shaping the granite with his bare hands and you can't see the face?

KEIGHLEY. Whose face is it?

HEBDEN. His face.

KEIGHLEY. Your face?

HEBDEN. Hicks's face.

KEIGHLEY. Hicks's face?

HEBDEN. His face is Hicks's face. He is Hicks. Once he tried to be somebody else, tried to mingle with the crowd, but he didn't belong down there. He was granite and he belonged up there.

KEIGHLEY. *(Returning to saucepan)* You've let this go all lumpy.

HEBDEN. To hell with that. *(Goes and looks up right)* He can't see the face himself now.

KEIGHLEY. It'll take time to make a face that size.

HEBDEN. He wants her to see it. He wants her to look up and see it out of her bedroom window.

KEIGHLEY. Have you written another letter?

(HEBDEN *takes letter out of clothes and holds it out to* KEIGHLEY)

KEIGHLEY. *(Taking letter)* I'll carry it down with me.

47

(HEBDEN *goes out with saucepan and haversack.*
KEIGHLEY *moves chairs, then returns to stage
right)*

16. MESSAGE INTERCEPTED

(PONDEN *stands on a step-ladder stage-right.* KEIGHLEY
*near steps paces up and down looking about as he does
so.* PONDEN *watches* KEIGHLEY. *Suddenly* KEIGHLEY
*draws letter out of pocket and moves briskly away from
steps.* PONDEN *jumps on his back. They fall to the floor,*
KEIGHLEY *full-length,* PONDEN *astride him)*

PONDEN. Got you, my lad.

KEIGHLEY. You're squashing me.

PONDEN. I'd prefer it if neither you nor your friend
called at my house in the foreseeable future. She is
not well, she is not well at all and I'm afraid that the
sight of either of you would exacerbate her
condition. *(Seizes letter)*

KEIGHLEY. You're hurting me.

PONDEN. I'm told that your friend is living in a ruined
farmhouse on the moor and that you are working in
the town as a milk roundsman. I wish you'd both go
away. I wish you'd take yourselves off to some distant
part of the country and leave us in peace. This letter
doesn't appear to be addressed to anyone.

(PONDEN *gets up.* KEIGHLEY *sits up painfully)*

KEIGHLEY. Can I have it back?

PONDEN. No *(Tearing open envelope)* Perhaps there's
no letter inside.

KEIGHLEY. The letter's not for you.

PONDEN. Is it not? *(Takes out letter, glances at it)* Are
you aware of the contents of this letter?

KEIGHLEY. *(Shakes head)*

PONDEN. It was not penned by you?

KEIGHLEY. No.

PONDEN. *(Reads letter aloud)* 'When will you come to
him? He lives only in hope that you will make up your
mind to come. One day. He will wait here for that day,
however far off it may be. Meanwhile, look out of

your bedroom window, in the morning, when the sun shines on the crag. You will see his face gazing down at you. In the evening, you may see its shadow. He will wait here for ever, he will never budge. Come.' *(Looks up at stage right)* I see no face.

KEIGHLEY. It's not visible.

PONDEN. Your friend shows signs of being unhinged.

(KEIGHLEY *gets to his feet)*

KEIGHLEY. You've turned a bit nasty.

PONDEN. Have I? Have I?

KEIGHLEY. Jumping on people out of trees. A bit violent.

PONDEN. I've a lot to put up with. But that's no excuse. What can I say? My behaviour was indefensible, I must keep a tighter grip on myself. But that's no answer. These instincts should not have to be repressed. They should wither away as one becomes more mature.

KEIGHLEY. Yours are getting stronger.

PONDEN. Yes, it's alarming. I'm sorry, very sorry.

KEIGHLEY. I'm sorry for you.

PONDEN. Yes. Damn it! *(Strikes brow with hand, then becomes absorbed in re-reading letter)*

(KEIGHLEY *goes off,* PONDEN *remains looking at letter as tape plays)*

TAPE. Why does a faint smile play over my thin lips beneath the thin black line of my moustache? My eyes are occupied with the road ahead, my gloved hands rest lightly on the wheel, the car's bonnet reflects the wintry sunshine and a wraith of mist drifts across the anonymous acres of arable land to right and left. But with my mind's eye I am observing a curious domestic scene: the would-be professor is going through her désk, her wardrobe, her chest-of-drawers, even her empty suitcases. Dresses, coats, skirts, stockings, jumpers, underclothes, forgotten knick-knacks are scattered about the house. The professor has found what he was looking for. How energetically, how innocently, the poor rat runs his pre-ordained race.

(PONDEN *goes off)*

(PONDEN *enters up left with sackful of letters.*
HAWORTH *enters right)*

PONDEN. *(Pouring letters on floor)* What have you to
say? Your duplicity leaves me speechless. Have you
contributed to this passionate correspondence? Is
there, somewhere else, in some corner of the moor, a
pile of paper as large as this, but inscribed with your
handwriting?

HAWORTH. *(Shakes head)*

PONDEN. All the same, you've thought it worth pre-
serving and worth concealing. That's what rankles. Do
you want to join this madman in his windswept
shanty? Have I prevented you? I thought I was
protecting you from something you feared, I thought
you looked on these four walls as your home, your
sanctuary. Am I your jailor, then? Is this a prison?
If only you'd confide in me, discuss it with me, if only
you'd communicate like a rational being.

HAWORTH. *(Turns away)*

PONDEN. *(Walking through pile of letters)* As to more
practical considerations. What's to be done with all
this paper? We really can't continue to keep it in the
bottoms of drawers, behind cushions, under the
mattress, inside the pages of books. There's the fire
risk as well as the inconvenience.

HAWORTH. Burn it.

PONDEN. You want me to burn it? That might be the
best solution.

HAWORTH. Put them in the flames and push them in
with the poker.

PONDEN. Very well. But a thought occurs to me. We
have a poker, but no flames. The central heating
units would be useless, so would the electric fire.
The immersion heater will hardly serve, nor will the
electric cooker.

HAWORTH. Put them in the oven.

PONDEN. Would baking them be sufficient? Wouldn't
it simply crisp the paper and make an awful mess of
the oven.

HAWORTH. You'll have to light a bonfire in the garden.

PONDEN. I dislike bonfires. Particularly at this time of the year. The garden is not large. With all this paper, it could easily blow about the place and set light to something. Quite apart from the way our neighbours would find black smuts clinging to their clean washing.

HAWORTH. What are you going to do, then?

PONDEN. Suppose we tear them up into small pieces and put them in the sack for the dustmen to collect?

HAWORTH. If we can't have a fire, I'd rather keep them.

PONDEN. As you wish. But if you insist on keeping them, they will have to be put away decently, conveniently and neatly. *(He kneels down by the letters)* Suppose I were to file them for you? Are they dated? *(Picks up letters at random and looks at them)* Apparently not. And the general similarity of the style makes dating by internal evidence difficult. If I'm to index them at all, it will have to be by first lines.

HAWORTH. Most of the first lines are the same.

PONDEN. Damn! Could one do it by subject-matter?

HAWORTH. The subject-matter's all the same.

PONDEN. *(Trampling paper)* Damn it! Damn it! Damn it!

HAWORTH. Don't lose your temper.

PONDEN. I refuse to be beaten by this simple problem. There must be patterns of thought contained in these apparently random utterances. I shall study them more closely. I shall persevere. I shall get to the bottom of this man's mind if it kills me.

HAWORTH. I'm going to my room.

PONDEN. Do so, by all means. *(Sits down cross-legged and begins turning over papers and making notes in small notebook)*

HAWORTH. If you decide after all that you want to tear them up, I don't mind. They're not important to me now.

(HAWORTH *goes out*)

PONDEN. To me their importance is becoming more and more apparent.

(PONDEN *remains sitting amongst papers, reading, noting, stacking those he has read in neat piles*)

51

18. THE MEETING ON THE MOOR

(KEIGHLEY *comes in and stands behind* PONDEN.
PONDEN *continues to work on the letters)*

PONDEN. You're in my light.

KEIGHLEY.   This is what happened: she flung open her
bedroom window, smashed a pane, cut her palm.
Hauling herself on to the sill, she jumped, caught
the branch, slid down the tree, crossed the garden, the
road and a narrow stream. Climbing a stone wall she
began to run up the narrow, waterlogged path to the
moor. He, perched high on the crag, looked down and
saw her, jumped, landed on a fall of granite and
slithered in a scatter of stones. Picking himself up he
began to run with giant strides down the hill towards
her. She, three miles away, slid, sidestepped, balanced,
teetered, danced on the verges of the path, up towards
him. He rushed through furze bushes, sank in reedy
squashes, startled moorfowl, fell headlong over a
hidden boulder, picked himself up and ran. She lost
one shoe in a ditch, kicked off the other, tripped and
crashed sideways into a stream, picked herself up and
ran. He, his face and hands grazed and bleeding, his
clothes black with dust, patched with moss and peat,
and she, spattered with mud, her feet cut and bleeding,
her face, hands and hair also bloody, twigs of heather
clinging to her clothes, met behind the ruined farmhouse in that line of trees bent all one way by the
wind. They never spoke, but tore at one another like
wild beasts.

(HEBDEN *and* HAWORTH *enter at opposite
diagonals of stage, moving towards one another like
wrestlers in slow motion.* HEBDEN *seizes* HAWORTH
*by one arm, she gets hold of his hair. He bends and
throws her over his back. She takes him by one leg
and sinks her teeth into it. He falls sideways and
pushes her face away with his hand. She runs her
nails down his arm. He pushes her off with his feet.
She hurls herself on top of him. They seize one
another by the hair, the throat, the limbs, the
clothes, rolling and twisting this way and that, finally
subsiding into one another's arms and lying still)*

PONDEN.   My palms are sweating with excitement. The
mists are clearing. How is it that people think of
literary criticism as a dry job? It's a passion, an

authentic passion.

(KEIGHLEY *sits down near* PONDEN, *in profile to audience*)

19. THE LITTLE BLACK BURROW

(HEBDEN *stands up and goes to stage right*)

HEBDEN.   Kettle's boiling. Come indoors and clean up.

HAWORTH.   Indoors? Do you call that piece of driftwood a door?

HEBDEN.   Quite cosy inside.

HAWORTH.   *(Joining him)* It's like a little black burrow.

HEBDEN.   He had to block up the windows. You'll be glad of it when the wind starts to blow.

HAWORTH.   I don't like it.

HEBDEN.   You'll get used to it. Wait there. *(Goes off and returns with hurricane lamp)* Now you can look about you.

HAWORTH.   What is there to look at? It's a little black hole like somebody's outdoor privy.

HEBDEN.   Keeps out the worst of the weather.

HAWORTH.   What are those rags and tatters in the corner?

HEBDEN.   Bed-curtains. Make a lot of difference when it's draughty.

HAWORTH.   Ugh! What did I step on?

HEBDEN.   That's his bit of carpet.

HAWORTH.   Everything's damp.

HEBDEN.   Fire's a bit low at the moment. Wait till it blazes up.

HAWORTH.   I'm freezing.

HEBDEN.   It is nippy.

HAWORTH.   I don't like it.

HEBDEN.   There's a pan of porridge ready. *(Goes off and returns with pan and plate)* Wait till he gives you some of that for your supper. *(Ladles porridge on to plate)*

53

HAWORTH. No thanks.

HEBDEN. Come on, you need a bit of supper.

HAWORTH. Yes, but not porridge.

HEBDEN. It's all there is. He lives on porridge.

HAWORTH. I wish I was home.

HEBDEN. You are home. This is your home. Eat some porridge and you'll feel better. *(Holds out plate)*

HAWORTH. I hate it here. *(Knocks plate out of his hand on to floor)*

HEBDEN. What's the matter with you?

HAWORTH. I'm shivering cold, the lamp stinks, the floor's damp, there's an icy draught round the so-called door, those rags round the bed give me the willies, I'm bloody hungry, I loathe porridge and I wish I'd never come.

HEBDEN. Where did you think you were coming?

HAWORTH. This place isn't fit for sheep to live in. It's worse than prison.

HEBDEN. *(Smiles)* He had a dream once of being in prison. A dungeon it was more than a prison. His own dungeon. Jailor, he said, take me to see the deepest, darkest cell in my dungeon, take me to see the most miserable creature my dungeon contains. It's not a pretty sight, sir, said the jailor. I'm in a black mood, he said, I wish to view some wretch more hopeless than myself. Follow me, said the jailor. They went down stone steps. Deep into the innards of the earth. Water dripped from the ceiling, puddles stood on the floor. They came to a cell. The key would hardly turn in the door, the lock was stiff with rust. Look there, said the jailor and held the hurricane lamp towards something crouched in the darkest corner. Excellent, he said, grinding his teeth, his shadow thrown huge on the wall by the lamp, but is he wretched enough? Let us cut off his head in the morning. A chain rattled, I was reaching for his ankle. Thank you, I said, you've made me the happiest man on earth.

(Pause. HEBDEN *lies down)*

HEBDEN. He's tired. He'll sleep now.

HAWORTH. *(Squatting down and scraping porridge off floor)* I'm so bloody hungry.

(They remain in these positions)

20. THE TRUTH AT LAST

(PONDEN *lays out twelve piles of letters to form a clock-face with himself at centre.* KEIGHLEY *watches him from outside the clockface)*

PONDEN. What is the single most remarkable thing about this mass of correspondence?

KEIGHLEY. I don't know.

PONDEN. It's in the third person. *He is waiting* for her to come, *he* will wait for ever.

KEIGHLEY. He talks like that.

PONDEN. Very likely. And it's also indisputable that your friend actually penned the letters. This is your friend's handwriting?

KEIGHLEY. I'd say so.

PONDEN. Thank you. Nonetheless, these are not your friend's letters. Or, to put it another way, your friend didn't think of them as his letters. He wrote them on behalf of somebody else.

KEIGHLEY. Who?

PONDEN. Precisely. That is what we have to find out. Who is the real author of these letters?

KEIGHLEY. I don't know.

PONDEN. Think. We know something about the author of these letters, after all. He is not bound by time. He will wait for ever, he says, he will never budge. He is anchored in place, but not in time. What does that suggest? *(Pause)* Taken by itself, it suggests he's not human. The salient characteristic of a human being is his sense of time. Taken with the recurrent references to the crag, it suggests something else. That he's part of the landscape. The salient characteristic of a pile of granite is its confinement in space, its immobility. Now then, how, apart from writing letters, does your friend spend his time?

KEIGHLEY. Up on the crag.

PONDEN. Quite so. Your friend is trying to make that pile of granite resemble a human face, his own face. Why?

KEIGHLEY. I don't know.

PONDEN. Because your friend feels confined by his humanity, by his sense of time, and wishes to transfer himself to something not confined by time. He wishes to imprint himself on the landscape. And do you see what this means? It means she has made an elementary mistake in going up there to meet your friend. It wasn't your friend who invited her, it was your friend as proxy for the pile of granite. Your friend has lost all sense of himself as a human being. In trying to make the stone resemble a human face, he is inevitably turning himself to stone. The artist you see begins by shaping his material, but the material ends by taking possession of the artist. Now where does this bring us out?

KEIGHLEY. I don't know.

PONDEN. Bang in the middle of our previous discussion of *Wuthering Heights*. Humanity versus inhumanity. The artist personally may be on the side of humanity, but his work is not. And his work is the master. I've long suspected this. The essential inhumanity of works of art and literature. If we still persist in thinking of art as ennobling, uplifting, morally beneficial, this is only because first the commentators and critics and then the public at large are constantly altering the whole bias of works of art. This accounts for the uneasiness we all feel when first confronted by brand-new works of art—we can't help sensing their essential inhumanity. However, with the passage of years, the heroic and indefatigable commentators succeed in humanizing the inhuman, and so we're able to respond to the works of the past without dislike or anxiety. Plato was quite right: artists should be excluded from the ideal society, since they represent the fifth column of the inhuman.

KEIGHLEY. So what are you going to do now?

PONDEN. Fetch her home.

KEIGHLEY. At this time of night?

PONDEN. I shall take the car. We can drive up to within half a mile of the ruin and walk from there.

You'll come?

KEIGHLEY. All right.

PONDEN. *(Clapping him on shoulder)* Bravo!

(They remain where they are)

21. THE BLIZZARD

(HEBDEN *lying down,* HAWORTH *sitting in a hunch)*

HAWORTH. Christ, it's cold. I never thought it would
be like this.

HEBDEN. What did you think?

HAWORTH. I thought it would be a completely new
experience, a new life. Instead of which it's a much
damper, drearier, more punitive version of the old one.
I thought you'd be a magnificent, untamed, outdoor
revolutionary living in a cave. Instead of which you're
like an old nanny-goat living on a bombed site. I
thought we'd be standing up there silhouetted against
the sky, shaking our fists at humdrum humanity.
Instead of which we're all huddled up and shaking
with cold, wishing somebody would send out a
St. Bernard with a bottle of brandy. I'm going home
tomorrow.

HEBDEN. Home?

HAWORTH. Home, yes. Every lovely fitted bit of it.

HEBDEN. You hate that place.

HAWORTH. Compared to this, it's Paradise.

HEBDEN. Wind's getting up.

HAWORTH. Have you only just noticed?

HEBDEN. *(Putting hand on head, looking at hand)*
Snow. Where did that come from? *(Looks up)*

HAWORTH. There's a leak in your bloody roof.

HEBDEN. Not a very big one.

HAWORTH. In weather like this we could easily die
up here.

HEBDEN. Would that upset you?

HAWORTH. I suppose it never occurred to you to
consider my feelings when you kept bombarding me

57

with letters?

HEBDEN.   I knew my own feelings. I thought I could leave yours to you.

HAWORTH.   *(Standing up)* What's that? A light.

HEBDEN.   The end of the world.

HAWORTH.   It's a car, I'll swear. They've sent help.

HEBDEN.   *(Holding out hand)* You're right about the roof.

(They remain in these positions. KEIGHLEY *and* PONDEN *bring on two chairs, place them side by side, sit down, with* PONDEN *in driving seat and make movements of wipers with right arms, also swaying and jolting their bodies)*

KEIGHLEY.   It's a blizzard.

PONDEN.   Very thick.

KEIGHLEY.   I like snow.

PONDEN.   Yes?

KEIGHLEY.   Whenever it snowed we used to play a game. With toy-soldiers.

PONDEN.   I know.

KEIGHLEY.   We were the gods, you see, and they were. . .

PONDEN.   Humanity. Were your gods kindly disposed towards humanity?

KEIGHLEY.   They thought they were, but if they got bored, which they usually did, there was sure to be some war or other disaster to cheer them up.

PONDEN.   This is the end of the road. Make sure the window's closed. I'll leave the engine running and the headlights on.

(They stand up)

HAWORTH.   It's them! They're battling their way through wind and snow to our rescue.

HEBDEN.   He'll put the kettle on.

TAPE.   I'm growing strangely tired. All the mental energy I've expended on my shades—and suddenly I find that I've lost my appetite for their destruction.

58

Surely it isn't that I've come to like them? On the contrary! They hardly seem worth the trouble of crushing.

(HAWORTH *and* PONDEN *embrace centre stage.* KEIGHLEY *stands near them,* HEBDEN *further off, at right, with pan in hand)*

HEBDEN. *(After pause)* You'll want a nice cup of tea before you go.

PONDEN. How kind! But I think we'd better wait until we're home and dry, don't you?

HEBDEN. He'll have some in any case.

PONDEN. But you're coming with us.

HEBDEN. No thanks.

PONDEN. I insist.

HEBDEN. He's happy to stay here, thanks.

PONDEN. I wouldn't be responsible for leaving you here.

HEBDEN. You're not responsible.

PONDEN. No, but I must insist all the same. *(Puts hand on* HEBDEN's *arm)*

HEBDEN. Take your hand off.

PONDEN. Come along, there's a good fellow, we're all tired and cold.

HEBDEN. Take your hand off.

PONDEN. Now don't be a silly gubbins.

(HEBDEN *hits* PONDEN. PONDEN *reels back)*

HAWORTH. *(To* HEBDEN) You bloody animal. He was trying to help you.

HEBDEN. He's sorry. He's very sorry.

HAWORTH. Let him stay, if that's what he wants. It's his funeral.

(HAWORTH *starts to lead* PONDEN *away, but he suddenly twists back and confronts* HEBDEN)

PONDEN. By God, I'll not put up with your stupidity, your crass, dumb imbecility one moment longer. *(Hits* HEBDEN) Why must it always be me that turns

59

the other cheek? *(Hits him)* Why always you that offers the whining apology? *(Hits him)* Me that makes allowances? *(Hits him)* You that time and again brings the whole fabric of civilised society to the edge of catastrophe? *(Hits him)* Me that patiently repairs it? *(Knocks HEBDEN down)* Builds it again brick by brick. . .*(Kicks him)*. . .renovating. . .*(Kicks him)*. . restoring. . .*(Kicks him)*. . .building again. . .*(Kicks him)*. . .making allowances. . .*(Kicks him)*. . .missing time after time the chance of happiness for a generation . . .*(Kicks him)*. . .putting up with your insensate, insatiable, brutish folly. *(With a final volley of kicks, he leaves HEBDEN, turns and takes HAWORTH by the arm)* Come.

(KEIGHLEY stoops over the prostrate HEBDEN. HAWORTH and PONDEN stand near the chairs, stooped and hunched in the face of the blizzard)

HAWORTH. Aren't we there yet?

PONDEN. I can't understand it. I left the lights on.

HEBDEN. You'd better go back with them.

KEIGHLEY. I'll stay with you.

HEBDEN. Hear that?

KEIGHLEY. Lump of snow fell on the floor.

HEBDEN. She was right about the roof.

HAWORTH. But where is the bloody car?

PONDEN. I left it quite close.

HAWORTH. We've been walking and walking.

PONDEN. The lights were blazing. I can't understand it.

HEBDEN. That was a big lump. Didn't sound like snow.

KEIGHLEY. It was a slate.

HAWORTH. I can't go any further.

PONDEN. Must keep moving.

HAWORTH. Look!

PONDEN. The car! Thank God! But why no lights?

HAWORTH. To hell with the lights. We've found it.

PONDEN. What a relief!

HEBDEN. He's soaking wet.

KEIGHLEY. It's all this snow on the floor.

HEBDEN. Put him by the fire.

KEIGHLEY. Fire's out long ago.

HEBDEN. How can it be out?

KEIGHLEY. Smothered with snow.

(HAWORTH *and* PONDEN *sit on chairs*)

PONDEN. Battery's dead. That's why no lights.

HAWORTH. Can't you start it?

PONDEN. I believe it ran out of petrol. And then the lights drained the battery and so we're. . . *(His voice dies away)*

HAWORTH. We're out of the wind. I'm tired. *(Leans against* PONDEN)

PONDEN. *(Puts arm round* HAWORTH *and leans towards her)* Have to get out and walk. Have to. Fatal to sit here in this temperature.

(They don't move)

HEBDEN. What's that?

KEIGHLEY. Half a dozen slates.

HEBDEN. Roof's had it.

TAPE. Eyelids dropping. Head thick. Loss of concentration. Shades slipping. Very distant, very muzzy. Must put the final touches. No longer care. . .

KEIGHLEY. Those games we used to play when it snowed and we couldn't go out. . .

22. THE GODS DESPAIR

(HAWORTH *fetches toy-soldiers, puts them on stage in their usual positions. The others arrange the chairs round edges of stage. All four stand on their chairs)*

PONDEN. The gods have assembled in special session. Each god has been down to earth on a fact-finding mission. Each god has visited an island not his own.

HAWORTH. *(Jumping off chair and kneeling beside* PONDEN's *toysoldier)* I visited the Isle of Wight.

KEIGHLEY. What did you find?

HAWORTH. I found it had been re-occupied by the British. Apparently Alexander Dubcek's regime had offended all sections of British opinion. It was generally agreed by trade unionists, bankers, members of the Cabinet and Shadow Cabinet, backbenchers on both sides of the house, the press, the new left, the Tory backlash and a broad cross-section of average television-viewers and men-in-the-street that admirable as Dubcek's reforms were in theory, they either went too far too fast or not far enough too slowly. There was no violence. A small detachment of unarmed marines crossed the Solent on the regular ferry-service and the Isle of Wight was restored to British sovereignty.

KEIGHLEY. And Dubcek?

HAWORTH. Alexander Dubcek is sailing round the world single-handed forty-seven times without stopping. *(She lays* PONDEN's *soldier face down on the floor and returns to her chair)*

PONDEN. *(Kneeling behind* HAWORTH's *soldier)* I visited Cuba. After several invasions by both sides, the island is now jointly administered by the United States and the Soviet Union. Che Guevara is alive and living on a ranch in Mexico. He told me he hoped to return to Cuba, where every second child and every public building is named after him, but that he found it well-nigh impossible to get the necessary visas, American and Russian, at the same time. *(He lays* HAWORTH's *soldier face down on stage and returns to his chair)*

HEBDEN. *(Kneeling behind* KEIGHLEY's *soldier)* Wherever I went I found the world full of refugees from Guernsey. They assured me the island was now a barren wilderness and incapable of supporting life. However, on reaching the island I discovered a single inhabitant. Picking feebly at the stony ground round a withered tomato plant with the rotting horn of a cow, he claimed to be Trevor Huddleston. But so weather-beaten and emaciated was he that it was impossible to determine with any certainty his original race, creed or colour. *(He lays* KEIGHLEY's *soldier face down and returns to chair)*

KEIGHLEY. *(Kneeling behind* HEBDEN's *soldier)* The
Samoans politely directed me to the top of an extinct
volcano. There I found a strange creature imprisoned
in a stone jar, only its head protruding. The Samoans
worship this creature as a minor god, but whenever they
lay their offerings on the ground near the jar, they
say that the blurred features of the head seem to
wince with distaste. I asked the head straight out:
who are you? No I, it replied. Not Samuel Beckett? I
asked. Dust, it replied. *(He lays* HEBDEN's *soldier
face down and returns to chair)*

PONDEN. Alexander Dubcek. . .

(All clap hands slowly)

HAWORTH. Che Guevara. . .

(All clap hands slowly)

KEIGHLEY. Trevor Huddleston. . .

(All clap hands slowly)

HEBDEN. Samuel Beckett. . .

(All clap hands slowly)

PONDEN. You disappoint us.

ALL. You disappoint us.

PONDEN. We expected more of you.

ALL. We expected more of you.

PONDEN. But you're only human.

ALL. You're only human.

23. DEATH

(HAWORTH *and* PONDEN *on floor near stage-left.*
HEBDEN *and* KEIGHLEY *looking through 'window'
right. Same positions as for end of Scene 2)*

PONDEN. I used the wrong word.

HAWORTH. Vulgar.

PONDEN. Your book is so essentially human—yet I
think you were striving to make it inhuman. There's a
conflict there which you never quite resolve. But the
attempt to overpower the very powerful human
elements with the comparatively weaker inhuman
elements gives rise to occasional over-writing. But

63

who am I to judge?

(HAWORTH *points at* HEBDEN *and* KEIGHLEY.
PONDEN *turns to look at them*)

HEBDEN.   He's looking through the window into a
lighted room. He's more sad than angry. It's all plush
and cosy in there, fitted carpet, central heating, tele
and stereo, but the two people inside are quarrelling
over nothing. It's a sorry sight, he thinks, to see those
two caged people tearing each other apart in the
middle of all that gimcrack luxury.

(HEBDEN *lies down,* KEIGHLEY *lies across him, as
though fallen from a kneeling position.* HAWORTH
and PONDEN *sit on the floor side by side, his arm
round her, leaning together, eyes closed. Positions as
at end of Scene 22, without the chairs. The fallen
toy-soldiers remain centre-stage*)

TAPE.   They'll find me lying in the carcass of my costly
machine, rain driving through the shattered windscreen.
Lifting my cracked shades they'll be startled to find
my eyes wide open. They'll try to close them
without success. A cruel smile distorts my stiffened
face. They'll unearth the tape-recorder of course.
What will they make of my shades? Three women and
perhaps a fourth—a callow youth—glimpsed like a
reflection in the glass of the Trowell self-service
cafeteria, dead and cold these hundred years under
the snow, on the moor, at the foot of the featureless
crag, colossal, dark and frowning, swept by clouds,
swept by shades.

(*The curtains open to reveal the painting, with empty
holes for the faces*)

REMINISCENCES

We crept through a broken hedge, groped our way up the
path, and planted ourselves on a flower-pot under the
drawing-room window. The light came from thence;
they had not put up the shutters, and the curtains were
only half closed. . .ah! it was beautiful — a splendid
place carpeted with crimson, and crimson-covered chairs
and tables, and a pure white ceiling bordered by gold, a
shower of glass-drops hanging in silver chains from the
centre, and shimmering with little soft tapers.

Emily Brontë, *Wuthering Heights*

Charlotte: Oh! Suppose we each had an island of our
own.
Branwell: If we had I would choose the Isle of Man.
Charlotte: And I would choose the Isle of Wight.
Emily: The Isle of Arran for me.
Anne: And mine shall be Guernsey.
We then chose who should be chief men in our islands.

Charlotte Brontë, *Tales of the Islanders*

Papa bought Branwell some wooden soldiers at Leeds...I
snatched up one and exclaimed 'This is the Duke of
Wellington! This shall be the Duke!'

Charlotte Brontë, *The History of the Year 1829*

. . .a child's face looking through the window. . .I pulled
its wrist on to the broken pane, and rubbed it to and fro
till the blood ran down. . .still it smiled, 'Let me in!'

Emily Brontë, *Wuthering Heights*

Downstairs came Emily, dragging after her the unwilling
Keeper. . .growling low and savagely all the time. . .her
bare clenched fist struck against his red fierce eyes. . .

Mrs Gaskell, *Life of Charlotte Brontë*

Poor Hareton was squalling and kicking in his father's
arms. . .he carried him upstairs and lifted him over the
banister. . .he gave a sudden spring, delivered himself
from the careless grasp that held him, and fell.

Emily Brontë, *Wuthering Heights*

. . .in a stride or two was at her side and had her grasped
in his arms. . .she seized his hair. . .wrenching his head
free and grinding his teeth. . .he had taken her arm. . .I

saw four distinct impressions left blue in the colourless
skin.

> Emily Brontë, *Wuthering Heights*

In the dungeon-crypts idly did I stray,
Reckless of the lives wasting there away;
'Draw the ponderous bars! open, Warder stern!'
He dared not say me nay—the hinges harshly turn.

> Emily Brontë, opening stanza of *The Prisoner*

I have lost the faculty of enjoying their destruction, and
I am too idle to destroy for nothing.

> Emily Brontë, *Wuthering Heights*

His eyes met mine, so keen and fierce, I started; and
then he seemed to smile. . .but his face and throat were
washed with rain. . .I could not think him dead — I tried
to close his eyes. . .

> Emily Brontë, *Wuthering Heights*

The statuary found a granite block on a solitary moor. . .
he saw how from the crag might be elicited the head. . .
With time and labour, the crag took human shape; and
there it stands colossal, dark, and frowning, half statue,
half rock. . .

> Charlotte Brontë, 1850 Preface to *Wuthering Heights*

'It's like a colt's mane over his eyes!'. . .he seized a
tureen of hot apple sauce. . .and dashed it full against
the speaker's face and neck. . .

> Emily Brontë, *Wuthering Heights*

'Lo, this is human weakness. . .Brethren execute upon him
the judgment written!. . .! the whole assembly, exalting
their pilgrim's staves, rushed round me in a body. . . the
whole chapel resounded with rappings and counter
rappings. . .

> Emily Brontë, *Wuthering Heights*

The more the worms writhe, the more I yearn to crush
out their entrails.

> Emily Brontë, *Wuthering Heights*

I went round by the garden, and laid wait for the messenger. . .and we spilt the milk between us; but I succeeded in abstracting the epistle. . .'Oh, put them in the fire, do, do!' But when I proceeded to open a place with the poker, the sacrifice was too painful to be borne.

Emily Brontë, *Wuthering Heights*

DEATH OF CAPTAIN DOUGHTY

'The backward look behind the assurance
Of recorded history, the backward half-look
Over the shoulder, towards the primitive terror.'

T.S.Eliot: *The Dry Salvages*

DEATH OF CAPTAIN DOUGHTY was first performed on
28 March 1973 by Granada Television.

The play was directed by Carol Wilks and the cast was as
follows:

FRANCIS DRAKE	Jim Norton
CAPTAIN DOUGHTY	Terrence Hardiman
BREWER	Bill Stewart
VICARY	Malcolm Tierney
CHESTER	Antony Haygarth
BRIGHT	Roy Marsden
FLETCHER	Charles McKeown
FIRST SAILOR	Peter Gordon
SECOND SAILOR	Seymour Matthews
THIRD SAILOR	Paul Alexander

Designed by Colin Pocock
Produced by Jonathan Powell

Note. DEATH OF CAPTAIN DOUGHTY was
commissioned by Jonathan Powell for Granada Television
and was written and performed as a television play. In
writing it I deliberately set out (with the encouragement
of my commissioner) to explore the possibilities of
weaning television drama away from its addiction to the
clumsy excesses of naturalism, of discovering whether
the simplicity and flexibility of the stage might not also
be a virtue under the cameras. I see no reason why
DOUGHTY should not be done as a stage play, with a
minimum cast of six actors, and I publish the script in
the hope that some bold company will attempt its
first performance on the stage.   J.S.

PROLOGUE

(At the back of the stage, a large map of the Atlantic Ocean. Enter DRAKE)

DRAKE.   The wind commands me away. Our ships are under sail. God grant we may so live in His fear as the enemy may have cause to say that God doth fight for Her Majesty as well abroad as at home. Haste!

(DRAKE steps aside. NARRATOR enters)

NARRATOR.   Four hundred years ago Francis Drake sailed round the world. Queen Elizabeth and several members of her court were among those who put money into the expedition. The fleet of five ships, with one hundred and sixty-four men and boys on board, left Plymouth in December 1577; one ship, with some fifty men, returned to Plymouth in September 1580. Those who sailed from Plymouth included a party of gentlemen-adventurers, the chief of whom was a certain Thomas Doughty. Captain Doughty, who had helped get Drake his commission as leader of the expedition, did not return to Plymouth. This is a strange story, half light, half dark: we know what happened, but we don't quite know why it happened. We can see the facts, but we may miss the meaning. So we're going to tell the story as simply as we can, without dressing up, without disguising ourselves as men who have been dead for nearly four centuries. We are actors playing the parts of our ancestors. This is a stage or the deck of a wooden ship.

(NARRATOR steps aside)

SCENE ONE—PRIZE

(The other actors enter. One of them goes to the map and points out the Cape Verde Islands off the coast of North Africa)

NARRATOR.   January 1578. Drake captures a Portuguese cargo ship off the Cape Verde Islands.

(All the actors walk about the stage with a slightly rolling gait, as if exploring the deck of a ship. After a

73

few moments of this, DRAKE *stops and the others stop and look at him)*

DRAKE. A good big ship. Don't you like her?

BRIGHT. What's the cargo?

(DRAKE falls to his knees and slaps floor with the flat of his palm)

DRAKE. She's bung full of plunder. Feel her, feel her!

(All go down on knees and put hands on floor)

DOUGHTY. *(Pulling splinter out of palm)* Damned foreign hulk. The bitch doesn't like me.

BREWER. What's she carrying?

DRAKE. *(Caressing boards)* Silks, satins, fine fabrics, costly stuff for Portuguese ladies in Brazil. Sherry wine and madeira for the Portuguese gentlemen. *(Slaps floor again and looks round the others enthusiastically)* We'll take her, shall we?

DOUGHTY. *(Teasing DRAKE)* You are a real pirate.

DRAKE. *(Not taking it as a joke)* A pirate? I have the Queen's Commission.

DOUGHTY. Have you? To fight private battles with friendly states? To board and ransack foreign ships? We're not at war with Portugal any more than we are with Spain.

DRAKE. We're not at peace either.

DOUGHTY. Dubious, my dear chap, very dubious.

(DRAKE crawls rapidly towards DOUGHTY on all fours and stares closely into his face)

DRAKE. I am not a pirate, Captain Doughty.

DOUGHTY. *(Staring back)* Pirate is as pirate does, Drake.

DRAKE. *(Slowly and menacingly)* I am not a pirate.

DOUGHTY. *(After pause, lightly)* What's in a word? You are not a pirate. *(He smiles)*

(DRAKE relaxes immediately, changes to sitting position, puts hands flat on boards either side of his thighs)

DRAKE. I take this ship, her silks, satins, sherries and

madeiras, her officers and crew as lawful prize and
prisoners of Her Majesty Queen Elizabeth. *(Looks all
round actors as though expecting an objection)*

DOUGHTY. *(Still very lightly)* God bless her!

DRAKE. And I rename this ship. . .*(Thinks for a moment)*
. . .*Mary.(Looks challengingly at* DOUGHTY).

DOUGHTY. *Mary.* Excellent name. A touch Catholic,
if one wants to be critical, but then she's a Catholic
ship, after all. Or was until Her Protestant Majesty
took possession.

DRAKE. The prisoners will be treated with courtesy
until we can put them ashore at La Brava. The cargo
will be left under seal for the present. My trumpeter
Brewer and my brother Thomas Drake will sail in her
as officers. As commander of the *Mary* I appoint. . .
(Looks all round actors). . .Captain Thomas Doughty.

(Suddenly lunging forward, DRAKE *punches*
DOUGHTY *in the midriff, sending him sprawling.
Pause. Then all the actors get up and go off, except for*
DRAKE. *As he goes off,* NARRATOR *stops by map
and points to Cape Verde Islands)*

NARRATOR. Change of command at La Brava.

SCENE TWO—VALUABLES

*(*DRAKE *goes and looks at map.* BREWER *pokes his
head round one side of it and speaks in a hoarse
whisper)*

BREWER. General!

DRAKE. Who's that?

BREWER. It's me, General. *(Coming round map)*

DRAKE. Is Captain Doughty ready to land the prisoners?

BREWER. The man sent me to tell you so.

DRAKE. Let him go ahead then.

75

(Pause. BREWER *stands looking at his feet)*

Let him get on with it, Brewer.

BREWER. *(Taking* DRAKE *by the arm and leading him aside in a conspiratorial manner)* A word in your ear, General. Doughty's been tampering with the cargo. He's opened the wine. Not only that, he's lifted personal valuables from the Portuguese prisoners.

DRAKE. Did he drink the wine?

BREWER. We all drank it, seeing it was already open. But the crew don't like him. He opened the wine to stop them grousing.

DRAKE. Ask Captain Doughty to row over and see me when he's beached the prisoners.

BREWER. All of us serve *you*, General.

DRAKE. You serve Captain Doughty under me.

BREWER. Doughty doesn't think he is under you. He's not a sailor, he's not serious.

(BREWER goes off behind map. A moment or two later, DOUGHTY *comes on stage)*

DOUGHTY. Prisoners ashore and ship shipshape, if that's the correct expression. You asked to see me?

(DRAKE holds out his hand. DOUGHTY *takes it)*

DRAKE. *(Holding up* DOUGHTY's *hand)* These rings are pretty. *(He drops the hand and lifts the chain which hangs round* DOUGHTY's *neck, with a medallion at the end of it)* I never saw you wear this before. *(Their faces are close together in profile)* Whose ornaments are these?

DOUGHTY. The Portuguese gave them to me. I'm not a pirate, you know.

DRAKE. I gave orders the cargo was to remain sealed.

DOUGHTY. I passed on your orders.

DRAKE. *(Shouting)* Then who tampered with it?

DOUGHTY. Don't look at me.

DRAKE. Who then? The prisoners? The sailors? By God, Doughty, when I give orders I mean them. You're in command. Was the wine opened on your orders or against your orders? Lack of discipline either way.

DOUGHTY.   Don't let's lose our tempers, Drake. The culprit was your brother. Putting me in a difficult position. Your sailors are frankly scum. I don't mean that unkindly, but as a simple, factual description. They haven't had our advantages in life.

DRAKE.   Why did the Portuguese give you these valuables?

DOUGHTY.   The Portuguese officers are gentlemen. I liked them, they liked me.

DRAKE.   What did they get in return?

DOUGHTY.   Courtesy. Generosity. Mutual esteem. Qualities natural among gentlemen, far removed from any conception of material value, of mere gain or loss.

DRAKE.   These rings are of material value. You gained them and the Portuguese lost them.

DOUGHTY.   The rings are nothing in themselves. Outward tokens of the spirit in which they were given and received. Let me give one to you. *(Takes off ring and puts it in* DRAKE's *palm)* Let me give you two. There's a third. *(Puts second and third in* DRAKE's *palm)*

DRAKE.   And the dingle-dangle.

DOUGHTY.   *(Taking off chain with medallion)* By all means. *(Laying it on* DRAKE's *palm with elaborate ceremony)* With my profound sentiments, from one gentleman to another. *(Looking at the collection in* DRAKE's *hand)* In themselves nothing but shiny metal and coloured stone.

DRAKE.   For shiny metal and coloured stone like this scum go sailing and Queens fit out their ships. *(Closes hand over rings and chain)* Until further notice my brother Thomas will command the *Mary*, you will transfer to this ship, the *Pelican*, and I shall join my brother on the *Mary*.

DOUGHTY.   You're giving me command of the *Pelican* — the flagship?

DRAKE.   Command of the gentlemen aboard the *Pelican*, not of the ship. Obviously you're good

with gentlemen, not so good with scum. These
(Weighing valuables in hand) will go in the common
chest, to be shared out at journey's end between
Her Majesty and Her Majesty's pirates.

(DRAKE *goes off.* DOUGHTY *remains)*

SCENE THREE—DOLDRUMS

(All the actors, except DRAKE *and* BREWER, *come on
stage.* NARRATOR *goes to map and points at equator
half-way between Africa and South America)*

NARRATOR.   It took Drake's fleet a month to get over
to Brazil. Between the trade winds blowing from
the north and those blowing from the south
there's a windless corridor known as 'The
Doldrums'. Crossing the equator the ships were
becalmed.

*(All the actors lie down on the stage, stretched out
like landed fish)*

DOUGHTY.   Bad food, stale water, heat and boredom.

VICARY.   *(Propping himself languidly on one elbow
and looking off-stage)* Someone's paying us an
afternoon call.

DOUGHTY.   *(Yawning)* Who can it be?

FIRST SAILOR.   It's a boat from the *Mary.*

SECOND SAILOR.   It's Brewer, the General's trumpeter.

DOUGHTY.   Yap! yap! The General's spaniel. *(Sitting
up)* We should give him a warm welcome.

VICARY.   A kick up the arse.

DOUGHTY.   That sort of thing. *(To sailors)* Do you
know any rough seafaring games to entertain
comrade Brewer?

SAILOR.   A cobbey.

VICARY.   A what?

SECOND SAILOR.   A cobbey's a sort of. . .when he
comes aboard, you get a hold of him and . . .
everyone takes a turn. . .and. . .

DOUGHTY.   Most intriguing! Why don't you show us
the cobbey when our friend comes up the ladder?

78

(The SAILORS *stand up, dusting their hands on their trousers)*

VICARY. Nothing dangerous to life or limb, I hope.

DOUGHTY. *(Yawning)* I do hope not.

VICARY. You don't care?

DOUGHTY. One sailor more or less. Even God would hardly miss him.

(BREWER *appears, framed between the backs of two* SAILORS *waiting to receive him)*

BREWER. Captain Doughty? The General sent me over to see how you're doing.

DOUGHTY. Give the General's man a hearty welcome.

(SAILORS *seize* BREWER *by the arms, undo his belt, drop his trousers round his ankles, bend his head between his knees, then taking it in turns they beat his buttocks with their hands)*

DOUGHTY. We live and learn. *(To* VICARY) Won't you join in?

VICARY. I don't much fancy it.

DOUGHTY. We ought to muck in.

(DOUGHTY *goes and slaps* BREWER. VICARY *does the same)*

VICARY. How amusing!

DOUGHTY. *(To* SAILORS) That's enough. Let him go.

(SAILORS *release* BREWER, *who pulls up trousers and fastens belt)*

DOUGHTY. Take the General our warmest regards, Brewer. *(Lies down again)*

BREWER. I'll tell him what you think of him, Captain Doughty.

(The others also lie down, as BREWER *goes off)*

VICARY. So that's a cobbey.

DOUGHTY. Did you ever see such a dreary bit of

horseplay? But what can you expect? Ship's
biscuits, foul water and no wind. The seafaring
life. The cobbey's only an outward expression of
the bad taste in your mouth.

(DRAKE *appears at the back of the stage*)

DRAKE.   Captain Doughty! Put yourself forthwith,
bag and baggage, into a small boat and have
yourself rowed to the supply ship, *Swan*. Aboard
the *Swan* you're to take your meals with Captain
Chester and his officers, you'll have liberty to walk
about the upper deck, but you'll consider yourself
Captain Chester's prisoner. Understood?

DOUGHTY.   *(Screwing up his face, opening mouth and
wiping tongue with hand)* A very bad taste.

(All go off stage)

SCENE FOUR—STORM

*(Actors bring on a see-saw and set it on stage, if possible
against a large white screen, lit so as to throw huge
shadows of those on the see-saw on to the screen.
NARRATOR comes to map and points to River Plate)*

NARRATOR.   Storms and darkness off the River
Plate.

*(He goes off. DOUGHTY and CHESTER come
and sit on see-saw)*

DOUGHTY.   Captain Chester, you and I are rational
men. We know very well that these huge walls of
water, ferocious gusts of wind and worst of all
these miserable drifts of black fog have natural
causes. But I'll bet three-quarters of your crew
think they're supernatural.

*(They sway up and down on the see-saw at long
intervals, bending their heads as though against
lashing rain, speaking in loud, slow voices as though
against the din of a storm)*

CHESTER.   Very likely.

DOUGHTY.   Penalties sent by gods or demons for
sailing where we shouldn't sail, for going beyond
what's permitted.

CHESTER.   We're not the first to come here.

80

DOUGHTY. Not quite the first.

CHESTER. What? Magellan, do you mean?

DOUGHTY. Are you still there, Captain Chester? I can't see you.

CHESTER. Magellan wasn't lost on this coast.

DOUGHTY. *(As he goes down, he leans over the edge of the see-saw)* Christ, look at that sea! Like a mill-race under the poop. Gone again. Extraordinary.

CHESTER. What?

DOUGHTY. How even the most rational mind can give way to doubt.

CHESTER. What?

DOUGHTY. Terror. What if there was a black rock, sharp, coming at us out of the fog, submerged? Boom! What if the world were not round, after all? Do you believe it is? What if the world's actually a gigantic dinner-plate over which the ocean pours day and night like a mill-race into the black abyss?

CHESTER. The world is round. Don't worry.

DOUGHTY. We're told it is. What's the evidence?

CHESTER. Magellan went round it. Sailing westwards he came back where he started. Any rate the ship did, if not the man himself.

DOUGHTY. Do you believe in demons?

CHESTER. I've not met any.

DOUGHTY. Do you think it's just chance that everything's wrong with this voyage? First the calm, then the hurricane, then the fog, then the hurricane again?

CHESTER. Natural hazards.

DOUGHTY. Wouldn't you say Drake was losing his grip?

CHESTER. In what way?

DOUGHTY. His ships are scattered. Where's he making for? What's he after in these terrible seas, off these desolate coasts?

CHESTER. You mustn't lose heart, Captain Doughty.

DOUGHTY. Don't misunderstand me. I've seen books which tell you how to raise devils, how to make storms, fogs, calms, shipwrecks. It can be done. Men can command such things if they know how. Why is Drake's voyage going wrong? Don't you think it might be because he's annoyed somebody? Don't you think Drake and everyone who follows him might end up at the bottom of the sea if that somebody wanted to punish them?

(DOUGHTY's *shadow looms over* CHESTER's, *arms outstretched*)

(DOUGHTY *and* CHESTER *go off. Actors remove see-saw and set up mast at one side of stage. Or the see-saw and mast might be permanent parts of the set from the beginning*)

SCENE FIVE—GIBBET

(Actors come in and cluster round foot of mast. NARRATOR stands by map and points at it)

NARRATOR. On June 18th, 1578, Drake's fleet— re-united—dropped anchor at Port St. Julian, far down the coast of South America towards the Strait of Magellan.

(DRAKE *and* DOUGHTY *stand together some way back from the other actors*)

FIRST SAILOR. What is it?

SECOND SAILOR. Old mast. Spruce. Seen some weather.

THIRD SAILOR. This mast must have been Magellan's.

SECOND SAILOR. Magellan's? Why would he stick his mast in the sand?

FIRST SAILOR. Did Magellan land on this beach?

THIRD SAILOR. Fifty-eight years ago. He stopped to water and refit his ships.

FIRST SAILOR. Flagpole, was it? Did he put up his flag and it's blown to tatters over the years?

(They look up as if at the flag flapping)

THIRD SAILOR. I doubt this was his flagpole.

SECOND SAILOR. Maybe the ship's still under the mast. The sand covered it. If we dig down we'll come to the timbers.

DRAKE. You'll come to the bones if you dig down.

THIRD SAILOR. Bones?

DRAKE. Human bones.

FIRST SAILOR. Was this the cross to mark a grave?

DRAKE. It marks a grave.

SECOND SAILOR. Whose grave?

DRAKE. The bones of Magellan's officers are buried here.

THIRD SAILOR. How did they die?

FIRST SAILOR. Murdered by natives?

SECOND SAILOR. Fever?

THIRD SAILOR. Drowned?

DRAKE. Hanged. This spruce mast was Magellan's gibbet. From this gibbet he hanged his officers. Dig down and you'll find their bones.

DOUGHTY. Why?

DRAKE. They had no faith, Captain Doughty. They were afraid. Rather than follow their leader into the unknown they stirred up trouble among his crew. Therefore he hanged them for mutiny. *(Turning away from* DOUGHTY*)* Captain Chester, take charge. Fetch mattocks. Dig down. Let's view these bones. I want every man in the fleet to see a sand-strewn mutineer with his own eyes.

(DRAKE *walks away from mast.* DOUGHTY *follows him)*

DOUGHTY. You've made your meaning clear. Do we need this macabre exhibition? Even supposing they find a skeleton, it's more likely to frighten the stuffing out of your poor sods than stiffen their moral fibre.

DRAKE. This is where the real voyage begins. Poor sods are no use to me. I'm not asking more of Magellan's officers than they can still perform. We shall need blood as well as bones before we leave Port St. Julian.

83

(DRAKE *turns round,* DOUGHTY *with him. The other actors are standing in a group. Each holds a piece of bone so as to make a more or less complete skeleton)*

DRAKE. Behold the bones! And now you, Doughty, like these skeleton officers, must do some service to my expedition. You must stand your trial.

SCENE SIX—TRIAL

(Someone brings a stool for DRAKE. *He sits down with his back to the map.* DOUGHTY *stands at the foot of the mast. The other actors sit on the other side of the stage)*

DRAKE. This is the charge against you, Thomas Doughty: that you've done your utmost to discredit me personally and to sabotage this voyage.

DOUGHTY. This is a rigged jury and you are judge in your cause. If I'm to be tried at all, it ought to be in England according to English law.

DRAKE. The Queen's Commission gives me power of life and death.

DOUGHTY. Let's see it. *(Holds out hand and advances towards* DRAKE, *waving his open palm under* DRAKE's *nose)* Some commission that can make you one minute a pirate and the next a judge, just as the whim takes you. Let's see the amazing document. *(Still holds out his hand)*

DRAKE. Tie the prisoner's arms.

(Two of the sailors pull DOUGHTY *back to his original position and tie his arms behind him)*

DRAKE. We'll hear evidence. Brewer.

(BREWER *stands up)*

BREWER. The accused person, Thomas Doughty, when commanding the captured Portuguese vessel *Mary,* caused the cargo to be opened, distributed the contents among the crew and took valuables from the Portuguese prisoners, all against the express orders of the General.

DOUGHTY. Lies. You and the General's brother

84

were the guilty men in opening the cargo. As for the valuables, they were given to me quite freely.

BREWER. When the fleet was becalmed I visited the *Pelican* on the General's orders. The accused person, then in a position of responsibility on board the *Pelican,* had me beaten by all hands.

DRAKE. Why?

BREWER. Out of spite and revenge because it was I who reported his misconduct on board the *Mary*.

DOUGHTY. More lies. It wasn't my idea to give Brewer a cobbey. I never heard of a cobbey till that day. The sailors beat him and I took part only because I wished to show solidarity with my shipmates. The whole business disgusted me. But all this is too trivial to talk about.

DRAKE. Sit down, Brewer. Captain Chester.

(BREWER *sits.* CHESTER *stands up)*

CHESTER. While he was a prisoner under my charge on board the *Swan,* at a time when the fleet was scattered and subject to many dangers from wind and sea, as well as fog, Doughty went secretly among my crew trying to weaken their allegiance to the General and to sow doubt in their minds about the voyage. He even tried his tricks with me.

DRAKE. What tricks?

CHESTER. He suggested that he himself might cause the expedition to come to grief.

DRAKE. In what way?

CHESTER. I hardly know. I didn't take him seriously. He seemed to be claiming to have supernatural power over wind and tide.

DOUGHTY. Ludicrous! I merely told him I'd read books which professed to teach one how to raise winds and waves. I admit it was foolish of me to discuss such matters with an ignorant idiot.

DRAKE. Edward Bright.

(CHESTER *sits down.* BRIGHT *stands up)*

BRIGHT. I was walking quietly in the garden. . .

DRAKE. What garden?

BRIGHT. Your own garden, General.

DRAKE. At Plymouth?

BRIGHT. At Plymouth. And I overheard the accused person, Captain Doughty, talking treason. He said that Her Majesty the Queen and Her Majesty's Council didn't object to piracy, so long as they got a good percentage of it for themselves.

DRAKE. In other words he was saying they were corrupt and could be bribed?

BRIGHT. Right. He said they'd do anything for money. He also said that this whole voyage was a sham and a deception.

DRAKE. Did he say what he meant by that?

BRIGHT. The ostensible purpose of the voyage, he said, was for us to go round the bottom of South America and discover a new country there called Terra Australis.

DRAKE. True enough.

BRIGHT. But Doughty said that was all a load of cobblers. The real purpose was to sail up the other side of South America and singe the King of Spain's beard, burn his ports, burgle his treasuries and ransack his ships. But that was a deadly secret between the Queen and Francis Drake, because if the Lord Treasurer, Lord Burghley, got to hear about it, he'd stop the voyage altogether.

DRAKE. Why?

BRIGHT. I don't know.

DOUGHTY. Because, as you very well know, Drake, Lord Burghley is anxious to avoid a war with Spain. That's why he doesn't want you boarding Spanish ships and burning Spanish towns.

DRAKE. Did Doughty say anything else in the garden at Plymouth?

BRIGHT. He said that, in spite of everything, Lord Burghley knew perfectly well what was the secret purpose of the voyage.

DRAKE. That's a lie.

BRIGHT. I'm only reporting what I heard him say.

DRAKE. Lord Burghley did not know.

DOUGHTY. I'm afraid he did.

DRAKE. He did not and he could not. The Queen
herself, at our private interview, told me that
Burghley of all people must not be told the secret
purpose of the voyage, and this you very well
understood, Doughty.

DOUGHTY. All the same, he knew.

DRAKE. How could he know?

DOUGHTY. I told him.

(DRAKE *stands up in sudden fury and shouts*)

DRAKE. Out of his own mouth! Now you have it!
Bring in your verdict! Is he a traitor or isn't he?

(VICARY *stands up*)

VICARY. With all respect, General, as a trained lawyer I
must protest.

DRAKE. You're Doughty's friend.

VICARY. I don't deny it. I should think you might
allow him one friend among so many enemies.
These proceedings are illegal.

DRAKE. Who cares about the law? I know what I'm
going to do.

VICARY. That may be. But we can't be responsible for
taking this man's life.

DRAKE. You're not responsible for his life. Leave that
to me. All you have to do is say if he's guilty. Now
say it.

(VICARY *sits down. Jurors whisper among
themselves.* DRAKE *and* DOUGHTY *stare at one
another. The whispering stops, jurors sit rigid*)

DRAKE. Guilty or not guilty?

VICARY. The verdict is guilty. However we think the
the witness Bright is untrustworty since it's well
known that Doughty has frequently said that Mrs
Bright was a whore.

DRAKE.   Everything Bright said was perfectly true. I care nothing for Mrs Bright. I want my question answered: is this man a traitor?

JURORS.   *(Severally)* Yes.

DRAKE.   And deserves to die? *(Pause)* Raise your arms those of you who think he deserves to die?

(One by one they raise their arms)

DRAKE.   Then I pronounce you, Thomas Doughty, the the child of death.

(All go out, except DRAKE and DOUGHTY)

SCENE SEVEN—COMMUNION

(DRAKE and DOUGHTY kneel side by side facing audience. FLETCHER enters with Communion Chalice. He goes and stands by DRAKE)

FLETCHER.   The Blood of our Lord Jesus Christ which was shed for thee, preserve thy body and soul unto everlasting life. *(Gives chalice to DRAKE)* Drink this in remembrance that Christ's Blood was shed for thee, and be thankful. *(Takes back Chalice and moves across to stand beside DOUGHTY)* The Blood. . .

(DOUGHTY holds up hand to stop FLETCHER, then beckons him closer, FLETCHER stoops and puts his ear near DOUGHTY's lips)

DOUGHTY.   *(In absolutely level tone)* I was not a traitor. The trivial things I said and did may have been troublesome but were not treacherous. I told Burghley the secret of the voyage because I like passing on secrets, can't help it. Not intending to prevent the voyage. Besides it didn't prevent the voyage, did it? I stirred up the sailors because I like dominating people, particularly stupid people. I can't help showing off. Vanity, not treachery. I made difficulties for Drake because he's so serious-minded. People with a mission in life irritate me, I like to upset their plans if I can. Of course I never should have come, but I wanted to, I thought it would be amusing. It hasn't been very amusing. I wasn't a traitor.

FLETCHER.   *(Takes a step back and holds out chalice)*

The Blood of our Lord Jesus Christ, which was shed for thee, preserve thy body and soul unto everlasting life. *(Gives chalice to* DOUGHTY*)* Drink this in remembrance that Christ's Blood was shed for thee, and be thankful. *(Takes back chalice, as* DOUGHTY *wipes lip with back of hand)*

(FLETCHER *goes off)*

SCENE EIGHT—DINNER

(Actors bring in table with two goblets and a bottle of wine and two seats. DRAKE *and* DOUGHTY *sit down on opposite sides of table)*

NARRATOR.   Drake entertains Doughty to dinner.

(He and all except DRAKE *and* DOUGHTY *go off)*

(DRAKE *pours wine into both goblets.* DOUGHTY *stands up with goblet)*

DOUGHTY.   I propose a toast. You have a long and dangerous journey in front of you. Who knows what countries you'll come to, men walking on their heads, giants, pygmies, monstrous new animals; or what Spanish galleons you'll board at dead of night, what gold and silver you'll stow under hatches? How many of you will ever see Plymouth again? I drink to your journey, your discoveries, your treasure and your safe return. *(Drinks and sits down)*

DRAKE.   Thank you. *(Stands up with goblet in hand)* You also have a journey to go. Long and dangerous or short and easy? People, ghosts, monsters, treasures, torments? Only Magellan has been my way before, but it doesn't seem impossible. Every living man has been or must go your way, but it seems too dark and unreal even to think about. All the same I believe in God. I believe God will light your way. I drink to your journey and your safe arrival. *(Drinks and sits down)*

DOUGHTY.   Thank you.

DRAKE.   *(Puts arms on table and leans across to* DOUGHTY) I owe this voyage to you. You were the first to mention my name in high places. You used your influence to get this idea accepted.

89

DOUGHTY. *(Leaning across in turn)* I certainly owe
the voyage I'm going on to you. I'm sure you too,
since you believe in God, will recommend me in
that High Place.

DRAKE. I will, Doughty. Very persistently and regularly.
I shall not forget you.

DOUGHTY. You'll be sorry to lose me.

DRAKE. I will.

DOUGHTY. Why are you doing this to me?

DRAKE. *(Sitting back in chair)* It's necessary.

DOUGHTY. Why is it necessary?

(DRAKE *doesn't answer. Long pause, then*
DOUGHTY *speaks again, looking down into
his goblet)*

A very long time ago there was a war between
Greeks and Trojans. Remember? How it nearly
didn't happen at all, because the Greek fleet was
held up by contrary winds. So many quarrels
broke out among the Greek leaders during this
dreary period of waiting that the whole
expedition threatened to collapse and all the
Greeks were on the point of going home to their
farms. Remember?

DRAKE. I didn't have your education.

DOUGHTY. The Greek General was Agamemnon.
Obeying the will of the gods, he sent for his
own daughter Iphigeneia and slit her throat in
front of the assembled troops. Immediately the
wind changed, the fleet sailed and Troy was
sacked.

DRAKE. What about it?

DOUGHTY. You find human sacrifice everywhere, in
all periods of history, among all peoples. Abraham
and Isaac, the Crucifixion, and Cortes found it
among the Aztecs. Humans seem to feel an
irresistible need for it.

DRAKE. It was just the danger of mutiny. Discipline at
sea is a very delicate thing, more delicate than you
understood, Doughty.

DOUGHTY. And yet until we reached Port St. Julian

90

you hadn't decided what to do with me, if anything. Then you saw Magellan's gibbet. You talked about showing the sailors some blood, to impress them. But it isn't to impress the sailors. It's to satisfy gods that drink human blood.

DRAKE.   There are no such gods.

DOUGHTY.   No. And the world is round. Those are facts. But that's what it is to be human, after all, to know facts and live by fictions; to do frightful, unnecessary things and invent reasons afterwards to prove them necessary. The world is round, no question, but not when you're sailing round it. There are no gods that drink human blood, except when you think the gods may have turned against you. And then it's naval discipline. *(Raises goblet)* Good luck! I'm sure you'll make it home now, with my help.

DRAKE.   *(Raising goblet)* You too, with mine.

(DRAKE *and* DOUGHTY *go off. The actors remove the table and chairs)*

SCENE NINE --EXECUTION

(The actors come on with a block, which they place beside the mast, Then they stand aside in a small group and wait a few moments. FLETCHER comes on, holding a bible. He is followed by DOUGHTY and behind DOUGHTY by DRAKE. They pass in front of the map at the back of the stage. DOUGHTY suddenly stops and turns to DRAKE)

DOUGHTY.   May I speak to you privately? A moment.

(DRAKE *nods and* DOUGHTY *whispers in his ear, inaudibly.)*

FIRST SAILOR.   What's he saying?

SECOND SAILOR.   I can't hear.

(DOUGHTY *stops speaking to* DRAKE, *then comes and shakes each* SAILOR *by the hand. He pats* FLETCHER's *bible and shakes* FLETCHER's *hand. Finally he shakes hands with* DRAKE, *then he goes and kneels down at the block with his head upstage.* DRAKE *takes a long sword from one of the the sailors and goes and stands behind* DOUGHTY)*

DOUGHTY.   A word of warning: I have a remarkably short neck.

(DRAKE *raises the sword and brings it down.* DOUGHTY *drops his head upstage of the block.* DRAKE *turns to* SAILORS)

DRAKE.   Look! This is the end of traitors.

(The actors carry out DOUGHTY, *while* DRAKE *follows)*

SCENE TEN—SERMON

(FLETCHER *turns to audience)*

FLETCHER.   On August 11th, 1578, on Drake's orders, every man in the fleet made his confession and received the sacrament. I then mounted the poop preparatory to preaching my sermon.

(Actors enter and stand in a group facing FLETCHER)

My text taken from St. Paul's Epistle to the Hebrews, Chapter Twelve, Verse One: 'Wherefore seeing we also are compassed about with so great a cloud of witnesses, let us lay aside every weight, and the sin which doth so easily beset us, and let us run with patience the race that is set before us. . .'

(DRAKE *enters swiftly and pushes* FLETCHER *aside)*

DRAKE.   Thank you, Mr. Fletcher. Today I must preach myself. My text is this: if you think you've had a hard time up to now, you'd be better off dead like Captain Doughty. There are some people who are born, live and die as if the world were a garden and they had nothing to do there but flower, fruit and wither with their roots in fixed places and a gardener to tend them. There are others for whom the world is a formless chaos which, like God on the first day of Creation, they must wrestle with and make shape out of, in order that they may justify themselves in the sight of God and, when their own shipwreck comes, leave behind some small pennant over the waters of oblivion. I have set my hand to this voyage and my legs turn to jelly when I think of what I have taken on. I cannot conceive how we

shall do it, I tell you this frankly, I cannot imagine
how any of us will ever come out of it alive.

(Pause)

So, if anyone here wants to go home now, he's free to do
so. I'll put a ship at his disposal. There's my offer. But let
him find a good wind, because if that ship comes in my
way I shall sink her. Who wants to go?

(He hardly leaves a pause and there are no takers)

My second text is this: it makes me bloody mad to see
the stupid way you've been quarrelling among yourselves.
From now on every bloody gentleman is going to be a
bloody sailor and handle ropes and every bloody sailor
is going to handle ropes next to every bloody gentleman.
And in fact I hereby abolish the notion of gentlemen,
except as regards myself. I am the only gentleman here,
because I hold the Queen's Commission. *(holds up
document)* There it is! In virtue of this document I now
dismiss the following from their commands: Captains
Thomas, Winter, Chester and Moone.

(Pause)

CHESTER. Why?

DRAKE. Why what, Chester?

CHESTER. Why should we lose our commands?

DRAKE. Why not? My third and last text is this: Captain
Doughty was not the only one who deserved death. But
he will be the only one who suffers it. From this moment
we start this voyage afresh. In token of which I now
rename my flagship. We shall call her *The Golden Hind*.
And my new commanders will be the following:
Captains Winter, Thomas, Moone and Chester.

(He turns to go, then thinks better of it)

I will confirm to you the real purpose of this voyage. We
shall enter Spanish ports and burn them, we shall board
and capture Spanish ships, we shall carry their treasure
home to Plymouth. Not for the money, oh no. Though
God knows, we are poor enough to need it, and so is
the Queen of England. Why then? Because it is the will
of God that the old give way to the new, that the rich be
dispossessed by the poor and that what the Bishop of
Rome gives, an Englishman shall take away. Because
on this reeling globe God ordains constant change. What

93

you want you get and if, like Captain Doughty, you want nothing in particular beyond a little amusement, you will lose even that you already have.

(He goes out and the other actors follow him)